Waterfall Hikes
of
Upstate South Carolina

Revised Edition

Thomas E. King

**milestone
press**

almond, nc

Milestone Press, P.O. Box 158, Almond, NC 28702
www.milestonepress.com

book design by Denise Gibson/Design Den
www.designden.com

Cover photograph: Pinnacle Mountain Falls
All photographs are by the author unless otherwise indicated.

The quotation from "Falling Waters" by Glenn Oeland originally
appeared in the July-August 1990 issue of *South Carolina Wildlife*.
"Waterfalls, Ions, and Prozac" on p. 294 originally appeared in the June
2002 issue of *Backpacker Magazine* and on backpacker.com. Both
quotations are used here by permission.

Library of Congress Cataloging-in-Publication Data
King, Thomas E., 1945-
    Waterfall hikes of upstate South Carolina/Thomas E. King. —Rev. ed.
        p. cm.
    Includes bibliographical references.
    ISBN 978-1-889596-20-4 (alk. paper)
        1. Hiking—South Carolina—Guidebooks. 2. Waterfalls—South
        Carolina—Guidebooks. 3. Trails—South Carolina—Guidebooks.
    4. South Carolina—Guidebooks. I. Title.
    GV199.42.S58K56 2009
    917.46—dc22
                        2008023205

*This book is sold with the understanding that the author and publisher
assume no legal responsibility for the completeness or accuracy of the
contents of this book, nor for any damages incurred while attempting
any of the activities or visiting any of the destinations described within it.
The text is based on information available at the time of publication.*

Printed in the United States on recycled paper.

Falling Waters

Few sights captivate the eye like a waterfall. An irresistible magic draws us to gaze in wonder at these natural fountains. Waterfalls are among nature's most sought-after spectacles, attested to by the fact that many a mountain trail ends at the foot of a cascading stream. Their beauty and drama inspire poems of praise and tales of tragedy, and the danger posed by their perilous heights seems only to add to their allure.

Neither skillfully made photographs nor carefully chosen words can fully convey the beauty and drama of a waterfall. Scenes of such grandeur defy expression. Perhaps this is because a waterfall is as much an event as a place—the motion and the sound of falling water, the thunderous roar and drenching spray, the smell of fresh water on laurel-scented air—these delights must be experienced firsthand.

For untold ages, these places of wild splendor have beckoned from the ancient heights. Thanks to people who care, they beckon still.

—Glenn Oeland

Waterfall Hikes
of Upstate South Carolina

Thomas E. King

STATION COVE FALLS
OCONEE COUNTY

Table of Contents

Waterfalls of Oconee County 33
Oconee County Highway Map...34

Waterfalls of Greenville County continued

Waterfalls of North Carolina and Georgia 283

Appendices

Introduction

Waterfalls, flowing water, and quiet mountain trails calm and refresh the inner spirit. The loud crashing sound of water falling over a cliff and the quiet babbling sound of slow-moving shallow water in a creek evoke different emotions and reflections within each observer. The Cherokee Indians believed that the sounds of the falls and rivers were the voice of "Long Man," the god of the river, and that only the most spiritually aware, whose hearts and minds were attuned to Nature, could understand his language and the message he had for them in the sounds of the waters.

Waterfalls in the State of South Carolina are concentrated in the mountain counties of Oconee, Pickens, and Greenville. This area, including a few other counties, is known as the Upstate. This book gives detailed information about waterfalls and trails leading to waterfalls in Upstate South Carolina.

I have been hiking the trails of Upstate South Carolina and western North Carolina since the 1960s, and over the years I have found major variations among different trail guides—in trail lengths, waterfall names, waterfall heights, and hike descriptions. For example, in one publication, Opossum Creek Falls is listed as being 150 feet high with the trail listed as moderate. In another publication the same falls is listed as being 50 feet high with the trail listed as difficult. This book reconciles such conflicting data from several guidebooks. It also includes Upstate South Carolina historical, geological, and geographical information, along with a few legends and anecdotes and technical data about trails and waterfalls.

This revised edition includes 30 previously unlisted waterfall hikes rated from easy to strenuous. Many of these falls are located off established trails, and the hikes are rated difficult to strenuous, with bushwhacking and water crossings necessary. However, the reward is worth the effort. Heights of these newly included falls range from 6 feet to 100 feet, with most of them averaging 30 to 50 feet. Although the appearance of waterfalls is always subject to change, the data presented in this book are to the best of my knowledge current and accurate. I hiked to all of the waterfalls listed here during 2006 and 2007.

Since the purpose of this book is to encourage individuals, groups, and families to enjoy our trails and waterfalls, it features many easy-to-access waterfalls, along with those which can be observed, even photographed, from the comfort of one's vehicle while parked on the roadside or in a parking lot. What could be "easier"?

T.E.K.
June, 2008

Preparing for Your Hike

Using This Book

Each listing includes the following components:

- Waterfall **Class** indicates the type, or structure, of the waterfall listed—for example: fan, block, or plunge. For more on waterfall structure classification, see p. 23.
- Although rating the appeal of a waterfall is subjective, waterfalls have a **Rating** system for that as well. Each one in this book is rated nice, fair, good, excellent, or spectacular according to the rating system on p. 24.
- You'll find the **Height** listed in each waterfall entry. For more on measuring waterfalls, see "Measuring Waterfalls" on p. 25.
- Every waterfall has a source. **Stream** gives the body of water that forms the falls.
- **Hike Length** is the distance you'll need to walk from your car to view the falls. Some distances are as little as 10 feet. Remember to double the distance for a round trip.
- **Trail Difficulty** indicates whether the trail is easy, moderate, or more difficult. For detailed trail rating descriptions, see p. 27.
- **Estimated Hiking Time** is based on a one-way trip to the falls. You'll have to double the estimated time—and sometimes allow even more time—for a round trip. See p. 29 for more on estimated hiking times.
- **USGS Quad Map** gives the name of the U.S. Geological Survey topographical map on which the waterfall is located.
- If a **Fee** is charged to view a waterfall, it will be given here.

- **Abbreviations** used in this book are as follows:
  DNR—Department of Natural Resources
  FS—Forest Service Road
  N/A—Not applicable
  SP—State Park
  USDA—United States Department of Agriculture
  USGS—United States Geological Survey

Minimum Hiking Equipment

Here is a checklist of the most common items recommended for a half-day warm-weather hike.

Footwear
- comfortable hiking boots
- woolen or synthetic socks

Outerwear
- synthetic long pants and long-sleeved shirt
- waterproof/breathable jacket
- cap or wide-brimmed hat
- poncho or other rain gear

Food and Drink
- lunch/snacks
- water (32 oz. per person)

Miscellaneous
- insect repellent
- compass and maps
- whistle
- walking stick
- pocket knife or multitool
- personal first-aid kit
- sunscreen and lip balm (SPF 15+)
- camera
- toilet paper
- day pack or fanny pack
- plastic bags to pack out trash

Staying on the trail to preserve the environment

When there is no trail to a waterfall, the USDA Forest Service, S.C. State Park Service, and other individuals and organizations generally recommend that hikers not leave an established trail to bushwhack to the falls or stream. Hiking off established trails can encourage erosion, damage wildlife habitat, and may be harmful to rare and endangered plants. In addition to protecting the environment, for our own safety it may be best to refrain from bushwhacking to remote falls. There are other concerns as well:

- Waterfalls located on private property, and those that require extensive bushwhacking to reach, are listed in this book only to catalog their existence. I would not want to see our wilderness damaged by fellow hikers and waterfall enthusiasts just because they read about a remote waterfall in this book and feel they must see it.
- In some cases, I have been requested not to include a particular waterfall for fear it would be spoiled by not-so-caring hikers, and I have honored those requests.
- Finally, directions to some falls on private property have been omitted at the request of the owners.

Waterfall Dangers

Waterfalls themselves present specific dangers. Rocks, roots, and fallen trees are wet and slippery. One inadvertent slip can result in an injury or a fatality. Several years ago a friend of mine slipped and fell over a section of Upper Whitewater Falls. He was fortunate to suffer only a broken leg and to have fellow hikers along to help him out of the falls, back up the trail, and to the hospital. Two weeks following that incident, a Clemson college student lost his life there. A sign at the viewing deck for Upper Whitewater Falls states that 16 people have died there. At other falls—Wildcat Falls, Reedy Branch Falls, and Little Brasstown Falls—there are crosses or memorial markers indicating lost lives. In 2005 a hiker fell and was killed near Misty Cavern Falls on the Ishi Trail. The same year another hiker was seriously injured at Wildcat Falls, and in April 2006 a 43-year-old man fell to his death at Twin Falls. *Always exercise extra caution and common sense around all waterfalls.*

Trail Cautions

All trails pose differing degrees of dangers. It takes only one twist of the ankle on a small rock to ruin a hike. Days and weeks can be involved in recovering from a serious fall.

Plants

The most common plant dangers are poison ivy, poison oak, and poison sumac. These vines have leaves in groups of three. Heed the adage, "leaves of three, let it be." Stinging nettle contains thousands of fine needles all over the leaves and stems, so beware of letting your skin come in contact with this plant.

Insects

Hornets and yellow jackets are the most frequently encountered stinging insects. Yellow jackets build nests in the ground beside trails, or sometimes in the middle of a trail, and are easily irritated. The hiker who passes first and disturbs the nest is usually the lucky one; the hikers who follow are more likely to be attacked by the angry yellow jackets. A hornet's nest hanging from a tree limb can be an interesting and tempting item to try to knock down, but leave it alone. Various species of seemingly harmless bees can be fatal if a hiker is allergic to bee venom. Someone in the hiking party should carry a first aid kit that contains the antidote to bee venom. Ticks are dangerous because they can carry Lyme Disease and Rocky Mountain Spotted Fever. Avoid both ticks and mosquitoes by using insect repellents and/or wearing long sleeves and long pants.

Snakes

Snakes usually pose little danger because they are more interested in getting out of your way than getting at you. The poisonous snakes in the Upstate region are rattlesnakes, copperheads, cottonmouths (water moccasin), and coral snakes. If you see any kind of snake, just leave it alone, and it will leave you alone.

Bears

Bears are seldom seen during the day, though they are present. If you are camping and do not store your food properly, they may sneak into the campsite at night and deprive you of your food for the next several days. The noise made by hikers is usually sufficient to scare bears away from the trail. An October 2005 bear hunt organized by the South Carolina Department of National Resources harvested 34 bears. The largest bear taken was in Pickens County and weighed 400 pounds; the average weight was 180 pounds. Several more bears were treed but not taken. The 2003 hunt yielded 55 bears, and the 2000 hunt yielded 42 bears.

If you are confronted by an aggressive bear, most advice says don't run. Stand your ground and raise your arms to appear larger than you are; shout or throw rocks at the bear. Some backpackers carry firecrackers or small guns that fire caps. Loud noises such as these will usually scare a bear away.

Weather

Always be prepared with rain gear, and wear synthetic, water-resistant clothing that wicks moisture away from the body. Avoid cotton clothing, since it is chilling when wet. When hiking around waterfalls, the water spray can wet clothing, and even in the warm weather of the Upstate the temperature can drop unexpectedly and cause a hiker to experience hypothermia, the sudden loss of core body heat. On a warm day, of course, a misty breeze caused by a waterfall can be wonderfully cooling.

If you are caught in a lightning storm—and there are many in the Upstate during the spring and summer—find shelter at the lowest possible elevation on or off the trail. Remove metal pack frames and stay away from streams and open areas.

Hunting

Hunting is allowed in many hiking areas. Be aware of the hunting seasons, and wear international orange vests and hats or other brightly colored clothing and packs.

Water

Avoid drinking any water from streams or springs unless you treat the water with a purifier or filtering device. Ground water, no matter how clear or inviting, can be infected with many forms of bacteria that can make life miserable. Carry enough potable water—at least 2 liters per person for a day hike—to keep yourself properly hydrated, even in winter. Drink the water slowly and periodically even when you are not thirsty.

Responsibilities of the Hiker

Each user of this book is responsible for exercising caution and good judgment. Always hike with a companion and use special caution around waterfalls. Stay off rocks around waterfalls, as they are moist and slippery even in the driest weather. Stay on established trails whenever possible. Off-trail bushwhacking is sometimes necessary for access to some falls, but should not be done without adequately marking the route with colored surveyor's tape. Knowledge in reading a topographical map and in using a compass or GPS system is sometimes required.

Private Property Issues

Some of the waterfalls described in this book are on private property where *No Trespassing* signs are clearly posted. Hikers must honor and respect the rights of these property owners and not venture onto posted property without obtaining an owner's permission. In some cases, it is not obvious that property is private. When in doubt, it is always best to assume that private property may be involved and act accordingly.

The developers, real estate agents, and individual property owners who gave me permission to cross their land and visit their waterfalls did not necessarily extend that invitation to everyone who has a copy of this book. When property owners requested that specific directions to falls on their property not be given, I have honored their request. *I assume no responsibility for the actions of any individual using this book and cannot be held liable for the actions of any individual who violates the rights of private property owners.*

THE REGION

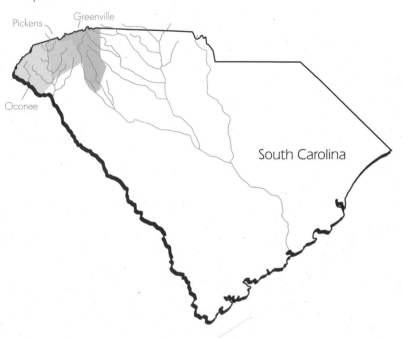

Upstate Counties

Pickens

Greenville

Oconee

South Carolina

Upstate South Carolina and the Blue Ridge Escarpment

Along the North Carolina–South Carolina border, Upstate South Carolina hosts a dramatic rise in the Blue Ridge Mountains known as the Blue Ridge Escarpment. An escarpment is a long, steep slope or cliff at the edge of a plateau or ridge, usually formed by erosion. The Cherokee knew the Blue Ridge Escarpment as "The Blue Wall" or "The Great Blue Hills of God."

This rugged and scenic escarpment rises abruptly from 900 feet in the foothills region to 3,554 feet at Sassafras Mountain, the state's highest peak. It comprises over 150,000 acres and stretches across

70 miles in the Upstate alone, with many more thousands of acres extending into North Carolina and Georgia. This tremendous sudden uplift of the mountainous region, coupled with an average rainfall of 80 inches per year, provides the area with one of the greatest concentrations of waterfalls in the United States. Raging whitewater rivers and calm mountain streams flow through this area, among them the Chattooga, Chauga, Whitewater, Thompson, Horsepasture, Eastatoe, and Middle and North Saluda Rivers. Many of the waterfalls in the Upstate are located on these rivers.

Waterfall Locations

The majority of the waterfalls in the Upstate are located in Oconee, Pickens, and Greenville counties. Oconee County has at least 85 waterfalls, Pickens County has at least 35, and Greenville County has at least 45. All of these counties also have numerous smaller, unnamed falls as well. The waterfalls listed in this book tend to cluster around ten towns: Clemson, Cleveland, Greenville, Pickens, Salem, Seneca, Six Mile, Tamassee, Walhalla, and Westminster. Oconee County, dubbed "The Golden Corner," derives its name from the Cherokee Indian word "Uk-Oo-Na," that has been translated in various ways, including "watery eyes of the hills," and "place of the springs." Many other names and traditions in the region have their origins with the Native Americans who inhabited this area. Table Rock Mountain derives its name from the Native American belief that gods ate from the flat top of the massive rock structure while sitting on a smaller nearby mountain called "The Stool."

According to legend, Hernando De Soto and his army of Spanish explorers passed through this area in 1540 and crossed the Chattooga River into North Carolina. Historians differ in their opinions of where De Soto actually crossed the Chattooga. Some claim that he followed the Indian Winding Stairs Trail that leads to Cherry Hill Campground north of Walhalla on SC 107 and then crossed the Chattooga River at Burrell's Ford. The Winding Stairs Hiking Trail is probably the path of an early stagecoach road. Others claim that he crossed at Nicholson Ford, a few miles south of Burrell's Ford. Legend claims that Juan Pardo, a member of the expedition, passed through Anderson County in about 1540. Others claim the De Soto expedition passed to the east of the Upstate.

De Soto was the first European explorer of this region. It was he who named the Appalachian Mountains—after the Appalachees, a tribe of Muskhogean Indians he had encountered in 1539 on the coast of the Gulf of Mexico.

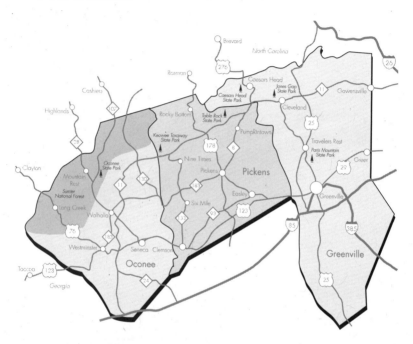

Public Lands in the Upstate

The major public land tracts with most of their acreage in Upstate South Carolina are:

Sumter National Forest	8,000
Ellicott Rock Wilderness	9,000
Table Rock State Park	3,000
Mountain Bridge Wilderness	13,500
Table Rock Watershed	9,800
Poinsett Watershed	19,300
Duke Energy Property	50,000
Total acres	112,600

THE WATERFALLS

What Is A Waterfall?

A precise definition of a waterfall is difficult to find. Most dictionaries and encyclopedias refer to a waterfall as a more or less vertical stream of water that flows over the edge of a cliff that has eroded away. A waterfall is also sometimes defined as a cascade of water crossing rocks that have not yet eroded, producing what is commonly know as a rapid. Different sources set different minimum heights, ranging from 5 to 20 feet, for water descending to qualify as a waterfall.

Other qualifying questions to consider:
- Must water constantly be flowing over the falls each day?
- What volume of water (e.g., cubic feet per second) is the minimum flow acceptable?
- What is the minimum degree or angle at which the water must fall or flow downstream?
- What is the origin of the waterfall—a constantly flowing stream, a spring from beneath the earth, melting ice or snow?

This book uses the following criteria to define a waterfall:
- A waterfall is a complete unit, sometimes composed of two, three, or more segments. Two segments miles apart should be considered as two separate waterfalls.
- Segments (each with a significant drop) only 10 feet apart can qualify as a section (for example, upper, middle, or lower) of the same waterfall. To qualify as a waterfall, one segment of the falls must be a minimum of 5 feet high.
- Most generally accepted true waterfalls must be located on a river, creek, or stream that provides an annual source of water.
- Most waterfalls have a significant amount of water flowing over

boulders or plunging down a cliff. However, some very low-volume waterfalls are attractive because of the shape of the rocks or the striations of color in the rocks over which the water flows. Such low-volume flows are called trickles.

One day a waterfall can be a gentle trickle of water gracefully gliding over the bedrock. The very next day after a rainstorm, that same waterfall changes its nature and shouts out its presence with a thunderous rush of water pouring over the rock.

Some people might say that the shoals, rapids, and low-flow trickles listed in this book are not waterfalls. However, based on my observations and information in other guidebooks, every waterfall listed meets the requirement of water dropping 5 feet or more in elevation over a very short distance.

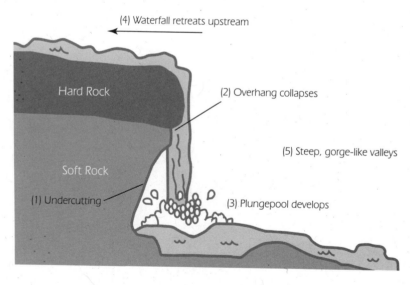

TYPICAL STRUCTURE OF A PLUNGE WATERFALL

Waterfall Structure and Classification

Waterfalls are classified into the following categories according to the physical structure of the segments:

- **Block**
  Formed by a wide flow of water extending uninterrupted across a river or creek.
  (Example: Reedy River Falls, p. 262)
- **Cataract**
  Typically occurring on torrents (large rivers), usually having a high volume of water.
  (Example: Riley Moore Falls, p. 124)
- **Fan**
  The falls widens at its base.
  (Example: Station Cove Falls, p. 136)
- **Horsetail**
  The water falls in a vertical drop and then makes contact with the rock surface behind the water, causing the water to spray out or change direction from the original path.
  (Example: Ashmore Falls, p. 210)
- **Plunge**
  The fall of the water makes no contact with the rock surface behind the water; also called a free-fall.
  (Example: Rainbow Falls, p. 268)
- **Rapids**
  A turbulent flow of water, usually through rocks, often navigated by whitewater rafters and canoeists. Rapids are ranked as Classes I through VI, in ascending order of difficulty. Rapids usually consist of less than a single five-foot drop.
  (Example: Woodall Shoals, p. 146)
- **Segmented**
  The water forms parallel drops where several streams (or part of one stream) fall over the same ledge side by side (twin, triplet, etc).
  (Example: Twin Falls, p. 194)
- **Shoal**
  Usually a stretch of shallow water characterized by visible rocks or sandbars under the water.
  (Example: Long Shoals, p. 172)

- Sluice (Chute)

  The water descends through a constricted passage.

  (Example: Chauga Narrows, p. 54)

- Tiered

  The water makes multiple drops over several sections of the falls (double, triple, quadruple).

  (Example: Whitewater Falls, p. 290)

- Waterslide

  The water glides down in a thin sheet over slimy or mossy rock slabs.

  (Example: Slickum Falls, p. 270)

Many waterfalls are combinations of the segments listed above. For example, Raven Cliff Falls (p. 260) is a tiered falls consisting of two plunges and a horsetail.

- Cascade

  A cascade is a generic term for any flow of water. A small creek can be said to cascade downstream over rocks. A cascading flow of water can be any height, from a few inches to several hundred feet. Each section of a waterfall is sometimes referred to as a cascade.

Rating Waterfalls

Waterfalls in this book follow the rating system below:

- Nice

  These waterfalls are usually small (5-15 feet high) with a low volume or trickle of water. May appeal only to serious waterfall buffs.

- Fair

  Small waterfalls (10-30 feet) on smaller streams.

- Good

  Larger and higher falls (25-75 feet). Usually very photogenic.

- Excellent

  Very appealing (50-100 feet). Considered to be beautiful. Very photogenic.

- Spectacular

  Impressive in size (100 feet and higher) and water flow. Ideal for viewing and photographing.

It's important to note that the pleasure afforded by waterfalls does not correspond to its rating. Rating a waterfall is very subjective. Even falls rated only fair may be very appealing, depending on the perception of the observer.

Measuring Waterfalls

Many criteria used for classifying waterfalls are subjective. For example, the height of a falls is measured from the uppermost precipice over which the water flows to the lowest point of contact in a pool or stream or over boulders. However, what constitutes the base of a falls is often a matter of opinion. Certainly most reported heights of waterfalls are only estimates. Even if the height were measured with sophisticated devices, the actual top and bottom of the falls would have to be identified before measuring, and sometimes this is not possible.

Photographing Waterfalls

Waterfalls are among the most popular photographic subjects. A photograph provides an excellent record of an outing, and the inclusion of people in waterfall photos indicates scale for judging the size of the falls. Almost any automatic, digital, or manual camera used today will produce an acceptable photo of a waterfall, but some knowledge of photography and photo techniques can produce a better picture.

Contrary to popular belief, the best time to photograph waterfalls is not on a clear, bright, sunny day. Most waterfalls have sections that are deeply shaded while other sections are brightly lit. Bright sunlight produces too much contrast between the highlights and shadows, so the best days for photographing waterfalls are cloudy and overcast. The cloud layer acts as a diffuser of light, filling in the shadows to produce a more evenly lit scene.

The use of filters, such as a polarizing filter and a neutral-density filter, can also help produce a quality photo. A slow shutter speed can enhance the water image by producing a smooth effect that gives the illusion of flowing water. A tripod is necessary when using slow shutter speeds.

Some waterfalls cannot be photographed in their entirety because of overhanging limbs and vegetation. Some must be photographed from a position in a river or stream that can be hazardous to reach.

In preparing this book, I looked at waterfall photos made as early as 1965. Some of the falls in those photographs are not accessible for photography today because the trails and/or falls are overgrown. One example is Fish Hatchery Falls, the 30-foot falls located one mile from the Walhalla Fish Hatchery on the East Fork Trail, which is no longer completely visible from the trail.

I have attempted to provide a photograph of acceptable quality with each waterfall description. These photos are not intended to be artistic statements. Instead, each pictures issues a call, saying, "Here's a waterfall. It is there to visit, view, enjoy, and refresh your spirit by its natural splendor. Determine the meaning of the falls for you, and apply that meaning to your life. Behold the unique form and beauty of this falls, which makes it different from all others."

Finally, be aware that embarking on a program of visiting and photographing waterfalls can become a time- and effort-consuming addiction for which there is no known cure.

Other Waterfalls in Upstate South Carolina

Some waterfall guidebooks list over 150 waterfalls in Upstate South Carolina. Falls that are accessible only by hikes 10 miles or longer, by very difficult trails, or by boat are not listed in this book. Other falls are omitted because there are no trails to them or they are on private property. Significant falls not included here are Bad Creek Falls, Hal's Falls, Headforemost Falls, Hurricane Falls, Jim Lee Falls, Moody Branch Falls, and Wright's Creek Falls.

Waterfall Hubs

Sometimes it is useful to plan trips around a waterfall "hub," a central point such as a city or along a major highway or near a state park. A list of waterfall hubs is provided in Appendix B.

The Hikes

Rating Trail Difficulty

Trail difficulty is based on variables such as elevation gain, steepness or grade, length, trail condition, and the presence of rocks and roots, overhanging ledges, and other features. A trail to a waterfall may be easy until the final approach to the falls, at which point it may ascend or descend steeply, requiring the hiker to climb over large rocks and boulders.

Perhaps the two most important elements in establishing the difficulty of a trail are its elevation gain and length. The steepness or grade of a trail is a third major factor in determining the degree of difficulty. Grades of one percent are wheelchair accessible. The easiest trails have grades up to 12 percent. From 12 percent upward, trails are rated as moderate to strenuous.

The difficulty rating system used in this book follows what I believe to be generally accepted, based on what a person in average physical condition might experience.

- **Easy**
  The trail is level to slightly ascending/descending. These trails are generally flat with few roots or rocks to impede steps and range in distance up to one mile. Some of the trails in this category are asphalt, concrete, or hard packed soil/gravel. Others may have steep and narrow and/or wet and slippery sections, and some begin on a wide gravel roadbed and then narrow to one or two feet wide over rocks and roots. Anyone with average health and stamina can negotiate these trails, and, taking time as necessary, should be successful in reaching a good observation point for each waterfall. Children are comfortable on these trails.

- **Moderate**

  Sections of the trail ascend/descend moderately, and negotiating roots and rocks will require moderate coordination and balance. Although these trails demand more effort, and some hikers will need to rest before reaching the end of the trail, those in good physical condition should have little difficulty. The length of these trails typically ranges from one to five miles. Children should be supervised closely.

- **Difficult**

  Many sections of the trail ascend/descend. A typical length would be three or more miles, although some trails of only one to two miles may be rated difficult because of rapid elevation gain. Still more effort is required, and experience is needed to negotiate steep ascents/descents. Several rest breaks may be necessary. Very good physical condition and stamina are required.

- **Strenuous**

  Sections of the trail ascend/descend steeply. Roots and rocks require great skill to negotiate. Some trails are rated strenuous because of their length, which in this category typically exceeds four miles. Excellent physical condition, stamina, and hiking experience are necessary. Strenuous trails are not recommended for children.

Some trail guidebooks and postings at trailheads use a combination of the above ratings, for example, moderately difficult, very difficult, moderately strenuous, or very strenuous. An unrated trail will be almost flat.

Even if a trail is rated easy, never forget that all trails in Upstate South Carolina are mountainous. A trail rated easy may have an area of steep ascent/descent, with large rocks and roots. Although intended to facilitate hiking on a steep trail, manmade steps may have a rise of one foot or more, which is difficult to negotiate in one step. Many trails to waterfalls require water crossings. Most crossings along the trails have footbridges, some with handrails, and are easy to negotiate. Others require rockhopping on unstable rocks and can be hazardous. In some cases it is necessary to wade across a creek. Be prepared with appropriate shoes for walking on slippery and sharp rocks under the water. Trails listed as easy in this book involve minimal water crossings. Trails listed as moderate, difficult, and strenuous may involve water crossings of varying difficulty.

Rating systems are somewhat subjective, and each person should seriously assess his/her own strengths and weaknesses before hiking any trail.

Estimated Hiking Times

The actual time required to hike on any given trail depends on many factors: the physical condition of the hiker, difficulty of the trail, weather, and temperature, for example. *All the hiking times listed in this book reflect distances one way.*

Many waterfall trails descend to and ascend from the falls back to the point of origin. Typically, the descent to the falls takes less time than the return ascent; the return may take twice as much time if the trail ascends. Keep this in mind and budget more time for the return trip.

For the novice hiker in average condition with minimum hiking/walking experience, the following times, which do not include rest stops, can be used as a general guideline.

Total Hiking Distance	Trip Estimated Hiking Time
0.5 mile	1 hour
1 mile	1 to 1.5 hours
1.5 miles	1.5 to 2 hours
2 miles	2 to 3 hours
3 miles	half day
5 miles	full day

United States Geological Service Quadrangle Maps

The USGS publishes 7.5-minute by 7.5-minute topographic maps which may help some hikers locate waterfalls and mountain trails. Because trails (and some Forest Service roads) are rerouted more frequently than the topo maps are updated, the information on the maps may be out of date. In each waterfall entry in this book, the name of the USGS Quadrangle Map which shows its location is provided. These maps can be purchased at map stores, sporting good stores, and hiking and outfitter stores, as well as directly from the USGS. You can write to the Geological Survey at 25286, Federal Center, Denver, CO 80225, call

303-236-7277, or visit www.topomaps.usgs.gov or www.store.usgs. gov. Software versions of the maps for each state are available on CD.

Fees

Most waterfalls are located on land owned either by the U.S. Forest Service, the S.C. State Park Service, or by private individuals or organizations. The Forest Service no longer charges admission fees in South Carolina. However, it does charge $2.00 per vehicle in North Carolina at the Upper Whitewater Falls access. The South Carolina State Park Service charges $2.00 per person at state parks (Oconee State Park, Table Rock State Park, Oconee Station Historic Site, and others). As of this writing, the fee is $1.25 for seniors 65 and over, and no charge for children 15 and under. The fee to view Toccoa Falls is $1.00 per person.

Weather-Related Trail Damage

Some trails and waterfalls of Upstate South Carolina were seriously affected by two major hurricanes, Ivan and Frances, which produced severe storms and massive amounts of wind and rain in September 2004. Large fallen trees are still resting at the base of many falls. Recently downed trees and large boulders displaced in 2004 continue to restrict the views of several falls and in some cases have altered the falls themselves. Blown-down trees have been cleared off some existing trails, and other trails have been rerouted. Among these is the trail into the Eastatoee Creek Heritage Preserve, which was closed in September 2004 because of major damage from Hurricane Ivan. Located on this trail is The Narrows, an area where the Eastatoe Creek funnels into a roaring chute only a few feet wide. This trail was reconstructed and opened to the public in October 2006. Copious rains and mild temperatures during the winters of 2002 through 2006 has spurred growth of rhododendron, azaleas, and mountain laurel, further obstructing access to waterfalls.

In December 2005 a severe ice storm affected Upstate South Carolina, breaking tree limbs and uprooting large trees from the already waterlogged soil. During 2006 and 2007 the Forest Service, S.C. State Park Service, and DNR, along with volunteers like myself from various hiking clubs, cleared most of the damage from the trails.

Trail Blazes

Many trails are well-marked by signs, posts, and kiosks erected along the trail by the Forest Service or the S.C. State Park Service. Another standard method of marking the directions of trails is to paint a rectangle blaze on trees or sometimes large rocks. The color used to mark a trail is different for each trail in a given area. Most South Carolina State Parks use a system of 3.5-inch-square metal signs nailed to trees and color coded. An example of the diamond-shaped signs is shown below.

Driving Directions and Distances

Driving distances in this book are measured to the nearest 0.1 mile from the road intersection mentioned or an obvious landmark mentioned (remembering that odometers vary). In addition, the following basic starting points from specific towns may be useful:

- **From Westminster** in Oconee County, begin at the intersection of US 76 West and SC 183 near the western town limits of Westminster.
- **From Walhalla** in Oconee County, begin at the intersection of SC 28 West and SC 183, where 183 turns right (north) near the center of town, two blocks before the County Courthouse.
- **From Pickens** in Pickens County, begin at the intersection of US 178 West and SC 183 near the center of town .
- **From Cleveland** in Greenville County, begin at the U.S. Post Office on US 276 West/SC 11 South.

Waterfalls
of
Oconee County

FALL CREEK FALLS

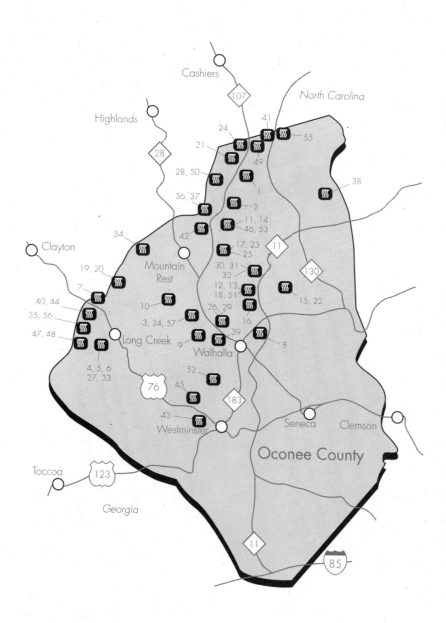

Oconee County is known as "The Golden Corner," deriving its name from the Cherokee Indian "Uk-Oo-Na." The word has been translated in various ways, including "watery eyes of the hills" and "place of the springs." Regardless of what its Cherokee name is, this place is known for its abundance of waterfalls. From the mighty Wild and Scenic Chattooga River that marks the border between South Carolina and Georgia to Walking Fern Creek near Cleveland, streams here offer spectacular waterfalls of all shapes and sizes.

FLAME AZALEA

Bee Cove Falls

Class:	Fan
Height:	40 feet
Rating:	Excellent
Stream:	Bee Cove Creek
Hike Length:	1.9 miles*
Hike Difficulty:	Difficult
Hiking Time:	2 hours*
USGS Quad:	Tamassee
Fee:	None

* one way

Bee Cove Falls is composed of four separate sections. They are usually referred to as Bee Cove Falls #s 1, 2, 3, and 4. The combined height of the four sections is approximately 130 feet; each section is separated by approximately 0.1 mile. Waterfall Section Heights are as follows: Bee Cove Falls #1–40 feet; Bee Cove Falls #2–30 feet; Bee Cove Falls #3–40 feet; Bee Cove Falls #4–20 feet.

The easiest to reach and the highest falls on Bee Cove Creek is Bee Cove Falls #1. It flows over multiple layers of granite, fans out at the base, and is forced through a sluice to begin the top of Bee Cove Falls #2. A large flat boulder at the base of Bee Cove #1 provides a place to relax and view the falls and is the precipice for Falls #2. The storms of September 2004 left many downed trees and other debris at the base of Bee Cove Falls #1 and the other sections. The lower quarter of Bee Cove Falls #1 must be viewed through dead trees and limbs.

Driving Directions:

1. From Walhalla follow SC 28 West for 8.1 miles and bear right onto SC 107 North.

2. Follow SC 107 for 12.4 miles to FS 702, a dirt road on the right. There is a small area for parking on the side of the road at the beginning of FS 702. This is the second road to the right after passing Fish Hatchery Road on the left.

Hiking Directions:

1. Follow FS 702 downhill for 1 mile to a crossing of Bee Cove Creek, which flows under the road.

2. Take the right fork of the road after crossing Bee Cove Creek.

3. Follow the right fork, descending for 0.5 mile to a 3-way intersection.

4. Take the road to the right over a dirt mound 3 to 4 feet high blocking vehicle traffic.

5. Follow the road 0.1 mile where the road curves to the left and a more narrow overgrown trail veers to the right.

6. Follow this trail to the right for 0.1 mile. Step over the fallen trees and branches. Rhododendron and other vegetation also encroach upon this trail.

7. Look to the left at 0.1 mile for a large white pine on the side of the trail and an obvious large, crooked chestnut oak a few feet past the pine.

8. At these two trees the sound of the upper falls can be heard to the left 300 feet downhill.

9. Leave the trail and begin the downhill descent walking to the right, upstream toward the sound of the falls. There may be some red and white surveyor's tape which will help lead to the base of Bee Cove Falls #1.

10. The other three sections of the falls are downstream from #1.

11. This trail is rated difficult because the Forest Service road and trail are downhill all the way, and there is no trail leading directly to the falls.

Big Bend Falls

Class:	Block
Height:	30 feet
Rating:	Spectacular
Stream:	Chattooga River
Hike Length:	2.7 miles*
Hike Difficulty:	Easy
Hiking Time:	2.5 hours*
USGS Quad:	Tamassee
Fee:	None

* one way

Big Bend Falls gets its name from the hairpin curve in the Chattooga River just above the falls. The water of the Chattooga cascades for 15 feet over a 30-degree, tiered rocky slope; then the water is forced between massive boulders creating a 15-foot block waterfall, the highest single drop on the Chattooga River. The water continues to flow over wide bedrock.

The shoreline of the Chattooga River below the falls provides small sandy beaches and large boulders on which to relax and picnic after the hike. The river provides some safe places for wading and swimming close to the shoreline. Because of the tremendous power of the water plummeting over the falls, the thunderous sound can be heard from the trail long before the falls is visible through the dense rhododendron, mountain laurel, hemlock, white pine, oak, galax, and thick green ferns.

Driving Directions:

1. From Walhalla follow SC 28 West for 8.1 miles and bear right onto SC 107 North.

2. Follow SC 107 for 8.5 miles and park at a pulloff on the right marked by several yellow posts. The parking area is just before the Cherry Hill Recreation Area. This is also the parking area for the Winding Stairs Trail and Miuka Falls.

Hiking Directions:

1. Big Bend Trail begins across SC 107 at a trail marker (a metal sign) posted eight feet high on a tree. The trail is sparsely marked with red blazes.

2. Follow this easy but narrow trail (with red blazes) 2.1 miles to an intersection with the combined Chattooga Trail and Foothills Trail.

3. Turn left at this intersection. (Twenty feet to the right at this intersection is a Trout Information Box used by anglers).

4. Follow this trail to the left, descending for 0.6 mile. (This trail soon becomes a wash with roots, rocks, and debris. Areas of the wash/trail after a recent rain will be slick with red mud). At 0.6 mile the shoreline of the Chattooga River and Big Bend Falls will come into view.

AMERICAN BEAUTY BERRY

Blue Hole Falls

Class:	Sluice
Height:	75 feet
Rating:	Good
Stream:	Cedar Creek
Hike Length:	0.5 mile*
Hike Difficulty:	Difficult
Hiking Time:	1 hour*
USGS Quad:	Whetstone
Fee:	None

* one way

Blue Hole Falls is one of several falls on Cedar Creek. The base of the falls and the large pool is 0.2 mile downstream from Cedar Creek Falls. The total cascade of Blue Hole Falls before it empties into the pool at its base is about 75 feet. The final section of Blue Hole Falls is a sluice into the pool. The falls gets its name because most of the time the large pool has clear blue water. A rainstorm can cause runoff that turns the beautiful blue water into a muddy brown.

The abandoned trail to Blue Hole Falls requires steep descents and climbing over ledges near the falls. The trail skirts a narrow ledge on the side of the falls and is wet and overgrown by vegetation. This trail is not recommended for the novice hiker; dense growth of rhododendron can make this a challenging hike. The knee-deep crossing of Cedar Creek between Cedar Creek Falls and the top of Blue Hole Falls can be hazardous.

When the wind is quiet and the lighting is ideal, the reflection in the pool mirrors the sluice and the steep slopes down to the water.

Driving Directions:

1. From Walhalla, follow SC 28 West for 6.1 miles and turn left onto Whetstone Road just before the Mountain Top Trading Post.

2. Follow Whetstone Road for 0.7 mile and turn left onto Cassidy Bridge Road.

3. Follow Cassidy Bridge Road for 0.9 mile and turn left onto Rich Mountain Road (FS 744, which is gravel).

4. Follow Rich Mountain Road for 3.2 miles and turn right onto Cedar Creek Road (FS 744C).

5. Follow Cedar Creek Road for 2.5 miles to FS 2658 on the right and park by an earth mound partially blocking the road.

Hiking Directions:

1. Hike 0.2 mile down FS 2658 to a T intersection. This stretch may be passable in a 4-wheel-drive vehicle.

2. At the intersection turn right onto FS 2656 at two large granite boulders placed on the roadbed to keep vehicles off the road.

3. Pass the first trail to the left, which ends at an overlook at the top of Blue Hole Falls. At 0.1 mile turn left onto the second trail (more of a wash), which descends for 50 feet to the crossing of Cedar Creek. FS 2656 ends at Cedar Creek 300 feet farther down the road.

4. Cross Cedar Creek at the base of Cedar Creek Falls and follow a very narrow trail for 0.1 mile that skirts the edge of the sluice and follows the right side of the pool about 20 feet above the pool. The trail is very narrow and dangerous as it follows the side of the pool above the base of Blue Hole Falls.

AZALEA

Brasstown Falls—Cascades

Class:	Tiered
Height:	50 feet
Rating:	Excellent
Stream:	Brasstown Creek
Hike Length:	0.1 mile*
Hike Difficulty:	Easy
Hiking Time:	15 minutes*
USGS Quad:	Tugaloo Lake
Fee:	None

* one way

Located in Brasstown Valley in the southern edge of the Sumter National Forest, Brasstown Falls tumbles 120 feet in three consecutive drops. Brasstown Valley extends southwest toward the Tugaloo River, which empties into Lake Hartwell. The Cherokee called this valley *itseyi*, or "place of fresh green," but early pioneers confused the word with *untsaiyi*—"brass." This misunderstanding continues today. Brasstown Falls consists of three distinct sections: Brasstown Cascades–50 feet; Brasstown Veil–35 feet; Brasstown Sluice–35 feet.

Access to Brasstown Cascades is a short, easy hike. However, the trail to the other two levels, Brasstown Veil and Brasstown Sluice, has steep descents and large boulders and is not recommended for the novice hiker.

Although often overlooked, the 40-foot Little Brasstown Falls is just a short distance above the three cascades.

Driving Directions:

1. From Westminster, follow US 76 West for 11.8 miles and turn left onto Brasstown Road.

2. Follow Brasstown Road for 4.1 miles (pavement ends in 2.6 miles) to FS 751.

3. Turn right onto FS 751 before a small bridge over Brasstown Creek and drive 0.5 mile to a parking area at boulders that block the road.

Hiking Directions:

1. Hike 0.2 mile down FS 2658 Follow the trail for 75 feet past the boulders at the parking area and pass under a power line.

2. Follow the trail for another 250 feet to a primitive camping area located to the left of the trail.

3. After the trail veers right past the camping area, follow it another 200 feet along Brasstown Creek to the first of the three sections, Brasstown Cascades, with a calm pool at its base.

JACK-IN-THE-PULPIT

Brasstown Falls—Veil

Class:	Block
Height:	35 feet
Rating:	Excellent
Stream:	Brasstown Creek
Hike Length:	0.2 mile*
Hike Difficulty:	Moderate
Hiking Time:	30 minutes*
USGS Quad:	Tugaloo Lake
Fee:	None

* one way

Located in Brasstown Valley in the southern edge of the Sumter National Forest, Brasstown Falls tumbles 120 feet in three consecutive drops. Brasstown Creek flattens out for a short distance before plunging 35 feet over Brasstown Veil.

Access to Brasstown Veil is a moderately difficult hike down steep terrain and over slippery rocks. The water falls in a wide pattern across Brasstown Creek and forms a 35-foot high veil of water before plunging into the swiftly moving creek at its base. This hike is not recommended for the average or novice hiker.

Below the veil, the creek narrows and the water is forced through a sluice into a pool. At the base of Brasstown Falls grows the rare dwarf filmy fern, a species rarely seen outside the jungles of South America.

Driving Directions:

1. From Westminster, follow US 76 West for 11.8 miles and turn left onto Brasstown Road.

2. Follow Brasstown Road for 4.1 miles (pavement ends in 2.6 miles) to FS 751.

3. Turn right onto FS 751 before a small bridge over Brasstown Creek and drive 0.5 mile to a parking area at boulders that block the road.

Hiking Directions:

1. Follow the trail for 75 feet past the boulders at the parking area and pass under a power line.

2. Follow the trail another 250 feet to a primitive camping area located to the left of the trail.

3. After the trail veers right past the camping area, follow it another 200 feet along Brasstown Creek to the first section, Brasstown Cascades.

4. Follow the trail another 200 feet to the second section, Brasstown Veil.

DEVIL'S BIT OR FAIRY WAND

Brasstown Falls—Sluice

Class:	Sluice
Height:	35 feet
Rating:	Excellent
Stream:	Brasstown Creek
Hike Length:	0.3 mile*
Hike Difficulty:	Difficult
Hiking Time:	40 minutes*
USGS Quad:	Tugaloo Lake
Fee:	None

* one way

Brasstown Sluice is the final segment of the Brasstown Falls chain.

As the water flows from Brasstown Veil, it is forced into a narrowing of the creek. The force of the water increases as it constricts and plunges 35 feet into a quiet pool. This shallow pool at the base of the sluice is suitable for cooling off on a hot summer day.

The trail gets progressively more difficult as it passes each section of the falls. Access to Brasstown Sluice is a difficult hike down steep terrain, along narrow ledges, and over slippery rocks and roots—not recommended for the average or novice hiker.

Driving Directions:

1. From Westminster, follow US 76 West for 11.8 miles and turn left onto Brasstown Road.

2. Follow Brasstown Road for 4.1 miles (pavement ends in 2.6 miles) to FS 751.

3. Turn right onto FS 751 before a small bridge over Brasstown Creek and drive 0.5 mile to a parking area at boulders that block the road.

Hiking Directions:

1. Follow the trail for 75 feet past the boulders at the parking area and pass under a power line.

2. Follow the trail another 250 feet to a primitive camping area located to the left of the trail.

3. After the trail veers right past the camping area, follow it another 200 feet along Brasstown Creek to the first section, Brasstown Cascades.

4. Follow the trail another 200 feet to the second section, Brasstown Veil.

5. Continue past the veil for 100 feet to the final section, Brasstown Sluice, with a pool at its base.

BEE BALM

Bull Sluice

Class:	Rapid
Height:	14 feet
Rating:	Good
Stream:	Chattooga River
Hike Length:	0.2 mile*
Hike Difficulty:	Easy
Hiking Time:	10 minutes*
USGS Quad:	Rainy Mountain
Fee:	None

* one way

Bull Sluice is a complex Class V rapids, and one of most dangerous on the Chattooga River. A paved trail leads part of the way to an observation platform from which you can often see expert kayakers and rafters negotiating its boulders and chutes. The rapids drop 14 feet, after which the water continues to flow swiftly, coursing downstream.

The power of the water makes this a dangerous place to try to wade or swim. Eight people—kayakers and others who simply were caught up in the water—have lost their lives at Bull Sluice.

Driving Directions:

1. From Westminster follow US 76 West 17.6 miles to the large parking lot on the right before the bridge over the Chattooga River.

2. Park in the parking lot on the South Carolina side of the Chattooga River.

Hiking Directions:

1. Follow the paved trail to the left of the "Information and Regulations" building containing information displays and restrooms.

2. The trail begins to the right of a large boulder inscribed "Wild and Scenic Chattooga River, May 10, 1974."

3. Follow the paved trail 280 feet.

4. Turn right onto a gravel trail. The paved trail turns to the left and leads down to a beach area.

5. Follow the gravel trail upstream 0.1 mile to a small platform overlooking Bull Sluice.

GREEN-AND-GOLD

Burnt Tanyard Shoals

Class:	Shoal
Height:	10 feet
Rating:	Good
Stream:	Little River
Hike Length:	N/A
Hike Difficulty:	N/A
Hiking Time:	N/A
USGS Quad:	Salem
Fee:	None

The 100-foot-wide Burnt Tanyard Shoals is on the Little River near Tamassee in Oconee County, located at the bridge on Burnt Tanyard Road. Although Burnt Tanyard Shoals may not appear to be a waterfall, it meets the criteria for a falls, as the river drops 10 feet here over a distance of 50 feet.

The fast flowing shoals is a favorite recreation spot for residents of the Salem/Tamassee area. On any hot summer day, many people can be found here wading, tubing, fishing, and relaxing among the large boulders and flat bedrock that line the banks of the Little River.

Driving Directions:

1. From Walhalla, follow SC 183 North 3.5 miles to the intersection with SC 11 and turn right onto SC 11 North.

2. Follow SC 11 North for 8.6 miles to the intersection with SC 130.

3. Turn right onto SC 130 and drive 3.3 miles through the town of Salem to Burnt Tanyard Road on the right.

4. Turn right onto Burnt Tanyard Road and drive 2.1 miles to the bridge over Little River.

5. Park on the roadside before the bridge and walk upstream along the shoreline to the shoals.

Hiking Directions:

There is no trail associated with these shoals. The shoals are visible from the bridge and the shoreline a few feet upstream from the bridge.

BEN GEER KEYS

BLOODROOT

Cedar Creek Falls

Class:	Tiered
Height:	10 feet
Rating:	Good
Stream:	Cedar Creek
Hike Length:	0.4 mile*
Hike Difficulty:	Moderate
Hiking Time:	30 minutes*
USGS Quad:	Whetstone
Fee:	None

* one way

Cedar Creek Falls is a 10-foot falls located 200 feet upstream of Blue Hole Falls, and it makes up for its lack of height by spanning Cedar Creek. When the flow of water is low, the rock face of Cedar Creek Falls can be seen. It is also possible to walk up to the falls on the bedrock below and wade in the shallow pools. This is a relatively safe recreation place when the water is low and the creek is calm. When the water level in Cedar Creek is high, the current is swift and water crossing can be hazardous.

While Cedar Creek Falls is an impressive falls on a swiftly moving creek, the much more impressive Blue Hole Falls is just downstream. The waters below Cedar Creek Falls begin the upper cascades of Blue Hole Falls.

Driving Directions:

1. From Walhalla, follow SC 28 West for 6.1 miles and turn left onto Whetstone Road just before the Mountain Top Trading Post.

2. Follow Whetstone Road for 0.7 mile and turn left onto Cassidy Bridge Road.

3. Follow Cassidy Bridge Road for 0.9 mile and turn left onto Rich Mountain Road (FS 744, which is gravel).

4. Follow Rich Mountain Road for 3.2 miles and turn right onto Cedar Creek Road (FS 744C).

5. Follow Cedar Creek Road for 2.5 miles to FS 2658 on the right and park by an earth mound which partially blocks the road.

Hiking Directions:

1. Hike 0.2 mile down FS 2658 to a T intersection. This stretch may be passable in a 4-wheel-drive vehicle.

2. At the intersection turn right onto FS 2656 at two large granite boulders placed on the roadbed to keep vehicles off the road.

3. Pass the first trail to the left which ends at an overlook at the top of Blue Hole Falls. At 0.1 mile, turn left onto the second trail (more of a wash), which descends for 50 feet to the crossing of Cedar Creek. Cedar Creek Falls is clearly visible upstream at this point. FS 2656 ends at Cedar Creek 300 feet farther down the road.

BLACK-EYED SUSAN

Chauga Narrows

Class:	Sluice
Height:	25 feet
Rating:	Excellent
Stream:	Chauga River
Hike Length:	0.6 mile*
Hike Difficulty:	Moderate
Hiking Time:	30 minutes*
USGS Quad:	Whetstone
Fee:	None

* one way

The Chauga Narrows is a unique feature on the Chauga River. Here, the fast-flowing water is squeezed through a narrow chute, dropping 25 feet over a 200-foot run and creating a Class VI rapids. Tremendous power is generated by the water funneling through the chute, yet at the base of the narrows the river calms to a pleasant fishing and wading stream.

The Chauga River is stocked with brown and rainbow trout, and trout have been seen trying to swim upstream through the narrows.

The trail to Chauga Narrows follows the calmly flowing river and offers many shoreline fishing opportunities.

Driving Directions:

1. From Walhalla follow SC 28 West for 6.1 miles and turn left onto Whetstone Road just before the Mountain Top Trading Post.

2. Follow Whetstone Road for 3.7 miles, then cross the river on Blackwell Bridge and park on the left side of the road.

Hiking Directions:

1. The trail begins at the parking area and follows an old roadbed for 0.3 mile. The roadbed is very rough with large pools of water during wet weather.

2. The roadbed turns into a narrow fisherman's trail through low-growing rhododendron and over slippery roots and rocks to Chauga Narrows.

FOAMFLOWER

Cheohee Road Falls

Class:	Tier
Height:	20 feet
Rating:	Fair
Stream:	Unnamed
Hike Length:	Roadside
Hike Difficulty:	N/A
Hiking Time:	N/A
USGS Quad:	Tamassee
Fee:	None

Cheohee Road Falls is a low-volume roadside falls flowing over black granite, located on Cheohee Road (FS 710) in northern Oconee County. Look for Cheohee Road Falls to the right on a curve after 0.4 mile on Cheohee Road. This road is also known as Tamassee Road and Winding Stairs Road.

This 20-foot cascade has little stream flow. The sound of the falls lets you know it is there, but the view is partially obscured by rhododendron and other vegetation. The best time to observe maximum water flow is after a period of heavy rain.

The falls is called Cheohee Road Falls because the water flow originates from springs and runoff higher up on the mountain and follows a natural worn path (wash) down the mountainside. The water passes under Cheohee Road through a culvert and empties into Wash Branch. Located another 0.4 mile down Wash Branch is the larger Wash Branch Falls.

Cheohee Road Falls may not be a final destination, but it is a refreshing site along Cheohee Road on the way to Wash Branch Falls, Crane Falls, and Secret Falls.

Driving Directions:

1. From Walhalla, follow SC 28 West for 8.1 miles and bear right onto SC 107 North.
2. Follow SC 107 for 6.1 miles and turn right onto Cheohee Road (FS 710, gravel). On some maps this road is named Tamassee Road and it is also known as Winding Stairs Road.
3. Drive 0.4 mile and look for Cheohee Road Falls on the right.

Hiking Directions:

There is no trail associated with this falls. It is located roadside and is partially overgrown with rhododendron and other vegetation. Listen for the sound of falling water at 0.4 mile to the right on Cheohee Road (FS 710), then look closely up the hillside for the falls.

BELLWORT

Connector Falls—Upper

Class:	Plunge
Height:	10 feet
Rating:	Nice
Stream:	Unnamed
Hike Length:	0.7 mile*
Hike Difficulty:	Easy
Hiking Time:	45 minutes*
USGS Quad:	Walhalla
Fee:	None

* one way

The recently developed 3.2-mile Oconee Connector Trail (part of the Palmetto Trail) crosses in front of this low-volume falls.

The waters forming this falls begin higher up the mountainside and plunge over this small rock outcrop with a small cavern behind it. The waters form a small pool in front of the cavern and then flow through metal culverts that were installed under the trail when the Oconee Connector Trail was developed. Large icicles and sheets of ice form around the falls in the winter. The falls has no official name, but it is a pleasant and relaxing sight on a relatively steep upgrade on the Oconee Connector Trail.

Before arriving at this small falls, you can hear a much larger falls to the right of the trail across a steep ravine. This falls appears to begin about 150 feet up the mountainside and flows toward the steep ravine. There is no trail established to the larger falls at this time.

Driving Directions:

1. From Walhalla follow SC 183 North for 3.5 miles to the intersection with SC 11 and turn right onto SC 11 North.

2. Follow SC 11 for 1.9 miles to the community of Picket Post.

3. Turn left onto Oconee Station Road at 1.9 miles.

4. Follow Oconee Station Road for 2.2 miles (0.2 mile past the entrance to Oconee Station State Historic Site) to a small parking area on the left.

Hiking Directions:

1. A well-established wide trail begins beside the kiosk in the roadside parking area.

2. Follow the trail 0.5 mile to a wooden stile. The Oconee Connector Trail to Oconee State Park (part of the Palmetto Trail) turns to the right at this point.

3. Turn right before passing through the wooden stile and continue 0.2 mile to Connector Falls on the right. The water from the falls flows under the trail.

FLAME AZALEA

Connector Falls—Lower

Class:	Tiered
Height:	30 feet
Rating:	Fair
Stream:	Unnamed
Hike Length:	0.7 mile*
Hike Difficulty:	Difficult
Hiking Time:	45 minutes*
USGS Quad:	Walhalla
Fee:	None

* one way

The recently developed 3.2-mile Oconee Connector Trail (part of the Palmetto Trail) crosses to the right of this low-volume falls. In dry weather the falls is not much more than a series of wet rocks on the mountainside.

The waters forming this falls begin higher up the mountainside and plunge over this rock outcrop beside the Oconee Connector Trail. During dry weather a thin film of water flows over the exposed rock on the mountainside.

The falls has no official name, but it can be heard and seen to the left of the Oconee Connector Trail during the winter after heavy rains. The falls is about 300 feet off the established trail and requires bushwhacking through many fallen trees and other debris alongside the stream and across the falls.

About 500 feet farther up the Connector Trail, a much larger falls (Don's Falls) can be heard and seen to the right of the trail across a steep ravine. Don's Falls appears to begin about 150 feet up the mountainside and flows toward the ravine; there is no established trail to it at this time.

My thanks to Scott Alexander, park interpreter at the Oconee Station Historic Site, for guiding me to this falls.

Driving Directions:

1. From Walhalla, follow SC 183 North for 3.5 miles to the intersection with SC 11 and turn right onto SC 11 North.

2. Follow SC 11 for 1.9 miles to the community of Picket Post.

3. Turn left onto Oconee Station Road at 1.9 miles.

4. Follow Oconee Station Road for 2.2 miles (0.2 mile past the entrance to Oconee Station State Historic Site) to a small parking area on the left.

Hiking Directions:

1. A well-established wide trail begins beside the kiosk in the roadside parking area.

2. Follow the trail 0.5 mile to a wooden stile. The Oconee Connector Trail to Oconee State Park (part of the Palmetto Trail) turns to the right at this point.

3. Turn right before passing through the wooden stile and continue 0.2 mile.

4. Look to the left through the trees for signs of a small waterfall. After heavy rains, listen for the sound of falling water on the left.

5. Bushwhack through a ravine on the left of the Oconee Connector Trail, following the small stream at the bottom of the ravine upstream to the sound and sight of the falls.

CATESBY'S TRILLIUM

Crane Falls

Class:	Fan
Height:	12 feet
Rating:	Good
Stream:	Crane Creek
Hike Length:	0.3 mile*
Hike Difficulty:	Easy
Hiking Time:	30 minutes*
USGS Quad:	Tamassee
Fee:	None

* one way

At the top of Crane Falls, Crane Creek splits, spilling its water down 12 feet, with half cascading straight ahead and half sluicing down the left side of the falls. The halves rejoin in a sandy and tree-limb-filled pool at the base.

An easy but overgrown trail, with three stream crossings, leads upstream to the falls

Driving Directions:

1. From Walhalla, follow SC 28 West for 8.1 miles and bear right onto SC 107 North.

2. Follow SC 107 for 6.1 miles and turn right onto Cheohee Road (FS 710, gravel). On some maps this road is named Tamassee Road and it is also known as Winding Stairs Road. It is very serpentine, sloping downhill all the way and looping back on itself several times.

3. Follow Cheohee Road for 3.2 miles to a bridge over Crane Creek. Pass Cheohee Road Falls at 0.4 mile to the right.

4. Park in the small parking space on the left before the bridge.

Hiking Directions:

1. The trailhead begins on the left at the bridge over Crane Creek.

2. Follow an old roadbed past several large barricading rocks and some primitive campsites.

3. Rock-hop across Crane Creek at the halfway point and follow the path upstream.

4. A number of downed trees and vegetation obscure the path on many sections of this 0.3-mile trail.

FROG'S BREECHES

DAR Shoals

Class:	Shoal
Height:	10 feet
Rating:	Good
Stream:	Flat Shoals River
Hike Length:	Roadside
Hike Difficulty:	N/A
Hiking Time:	N/A
USGS Quad:	Walhalla
Fee:	None

DAR Shoals is a turbulent, high-volume cascade dropping 10 feet as it flows over a 60-foot stretch of bedrock under the bridge over Flat Shoals River on Bumgardner Road. The shoals are located one mile off SC 11 in Oconee County.

The historic Daughters of the American Revolution (DAR) School was founded in 1919 by the South Carolina Daughters of the American Revolution at Tamassee and is located across the bridge over Flat Shoals River. The school was organized to provide an opportunity for children living in the isolated areas of northwestern South Carolina to learn the ideals of patriotism, citizenship, and spiritual growth. Both the shoals and the DAR School are inspirational and historical sites.

Driving Directions:

1. From Walhalla follow SC 183 North 3.5 miles to the intersection with SC 11 and turn right onto SC 11 North.

2. Follow SC 11 North for 5.1 miles to Bumgardner Road on the right.

3. Turn right onto Bumgardner Road and drive 0.3 mile to a pulloff on the right side of the road before the steel bridge over Flat Shoals River.

4. Park on the roadside before the bridge and view the shoals from the bridge.

Hiking Directions:

There is no trail associated with these shoals. For the more adventurous it is possible to follow the shoreline 200 to 300 feet downstream for a better view.

GALAX

Dick Lee Falls

Class:	Tiered
Height:	40 feet
Rating:	Fair
Stream:	Unnamed
Hike Length:	N/A
Hike Difficulty:	Moderate
Hiking Time:	10 minutes
USGS Quad:	Walhalla
Fee:	None

Dick Lee Falls is located on private property just outside the boundary of the Sumter National Forest.

Randomly scattered boulders across the unnamed tributary of Oconee Creek direct the water over and between the large rocks. The falls is about 20 feet wide. The base is cluttered with fallen trees, boulders of various sizes, and dense growths of rhododendron and laurel. After finding its way over the boulders, the water forms a pleasantly peaceful creek that empties into Oconee Creek 0.5 mile below the falls.

To reach the falls you must bushwhack down the mountainside through oak, hemlock, poplar, rhododendron, and laurel. Catesby's trillium and other mountain wildflowers populate the way to the falls.

Driving Directions:

1. From Walhalla follow SC 183 North for 3.5 miles to the intersection with SC 11 and turn right onto SC 11 North.

2. Follow SC 11 for 1.9 miles to the community of Picket Post.

3. Turn left onto Oconee Station Road at 1.9 miles.

4. The falls are located on private property about 3 miles down Oconee Station Road.

5. Specific directions to this falls are not given because it is on private property where several residences are located.

Hiking Directions:

There is no trail to this falls. It lies about 300 feet down a very steep mountainside behind a private residence. The top of the falls can be seen through the trees while standing in the backyard of the residence. The way downhill to this falls is populated with ferns and several varieties of trillium, along with other wildflowers. Be sure to ask permission before entering private property to get to the falls.

HAIRY SPIDERWORT

Disappearing Falls

Class:	Tiered
Height:	12 feet
Rating:	Fair
Stream:	Unnamed
Hike Length:	0.3 mile*
Hike Difficulty:	Easy
Hiking Time:	N/A
USGS Quad:	Tamassee
Fee:	None

*one way

Each waterfall is unique, but this one has a highly unusual feature. The small unnamed stream that parallels part of the Hidden Falls Trail can be seen and heard at several points. At 0.3 mile on the trail, the casual observer may see through the vegetation what appears to be a ripple in the stream and give it no further thought. Further investigation will reveal a 12-foot drop of water over a black granite rock. Then the water flows through a three-foot-wide slit in the ground, abruptly ends, and continues to drop about two feet under ground before leveling out and forming an underground stream. The ground at the base of the falls is solid with trees growing where there should be a stream, but the stream flows beneath the solid earth.

Driving Directions:

1. From Walhalla follow SC 28 West for 8.1 miles and bear right onto SC 107 North.

2. Follow SC 107 for 2.3 miles to the entrance of Oconee State Park on the right.

3. Continue 0.5 mile to Old Horse Bone Road (FS 716) on the right.

4. Turn right at the entrance to State Park Estates and take an immediate right (before the entrance gate) onto the gravel road (FS 716). Follow the road 0.9 mile, passing the barricaded road to the left that leads to the old fire lookout tower.

5. Turn right into the very short road, and park before the barricade.

Hiking Directions:

1. The trail begins behind the barricade on the short road where you park.

2. Follow the old roadbed from the barricade 125 feet to a sign pointing left to Hidden Falls.

3. Turn left and walk 0.3 mile on the Hidden Falls Trail.

4. Turn right onto a 30-foot path to the falls.

LANCELEAF VIOLET

Don's Falls

Class:	Tiered
Height:	50 feet
Rating:	Good
Stream:	Unnamed
Hike Length:	0.7 mile*
Hike Difficulty:	Strenuous
Hiking Time:	45 minutes*
USGS Quad:	Walhalla
Fee:	None

*one way

Don's Falls can be seen through the trees to right of the recently developed 3.2-mile Oconee Connector Trail (part of the Palmetto Trail). In dry weather a low flow of water courses over the exposed rock face on the mountainside. During the winter after heavy rains, the falls can be heard and seen to the right of the trail.

The waters forming Don's Falls begin higher up the mountainside and plunge over this rock outcrop beside the Oconee Connector Trail. The falls can be seen from about 500 feet up the trail from Lower Connector Falls. Don's Falls appears to begin about 150 feet up the mountainside and flows toward a steep ravine.

There is no established access trail; getting to it requires bushwhacking about 500 feet off the established trail, across a ravine and then up to the falls. The falls has been called Don's Falls for many years. According to local legend, it was named for the leader of a moonshine operation located there.

My thanks to Scott Alexander, park interpreter at the Oconee Station Historic Site, for guiding me to this falls.

Driving Directions:

1. From Walhalla follow SC 183 North for 3.5 miles to the intersection with SC 11 and turn right onto SC 11 North.

2. Follow SC 11 for 1.9 miles to the community of Picket Post.

3. Turn left onto Oconee Station Road at 1.9 miles.

4. Follow Oconee Station Road for 2.2 miles (0.2 mile past the entrance to Oconee Station State Historic Site) to a small parking area on the left.

Hiking Directions:

1. A well-established wide trail begins beside the kiosk in the roadside parking area.

2. Follow the trail 0.5 mile to a wooden stile. The Oconee Connector Trail to Oconee State Park (part of the Palmetto Trail) turns to the right at this point.

3. Turn right before passing through the wooden stile and continue 0.2 mile.

4. Look to the right across a ravine and up the mountainside; the rock structure of the falls is visible through the trees. After heavy rains, listen for the sound of falling water on the right.

5. Bushwhack through the ravine on the right of the Oconee Connector Trail and up the mountainside to the falls.

GALAX

Fall Creek Falls—Middle

Class:	Tiered
Height:	20 feet
Rating:	Excellent
Stream:	Fall Creek
Hike Length:	100 feet*
Hike Difficulty:	Easy
Hiking Time:	5 minutes*
USGS Quad:	Rainy Mountain
Fee:	None

*one way

Fall Creek Falls consists of three levels: upper level–35 feet; middle level–20 feet; lower level–40 feet.

This falls is located on Fall Creek Road north of Westminster, SC, in the Chattooga River watershed. The poorly maintained trail to this series of falls passes through dense growths of rhododendron, azalea, hemlock, and oak. The middle level, shown above, is easy to access. It begins at the end of the upper level. The third level requires bushwhacking an additional mile downstream. After plunging over the lower level of the falls, Fall Creek empties into the Chattooga River.

There are those who would say that the upper and middle levels are one waterfall. However, the physical structure and the 20-foot separation between the two sections make this two falls. The middle falls is also known as Andrew Ramey Falls Number Two.

Driving Directions:

1. From Westminster follow US 76 West for 16.4 miles and turn right onto Chattooga Ridge Road.

2. Follow Chattooga Ridge Road for 2 miles to Fall Creek Road (FS 722) and turn left onto Fall Creek Road.

3. Follow Fall Creek Road (FS 722) for 0.3 mile to a left turn.

4. Turn left and follow FS 722 for 0.5 mile, where the road crosses over Fall Creek. Four yellow-and-black diagonally striped road signs indicate that the creek crosses under the road. Park on the roadside, where you can hear the upper level of the falls on the left.

Hiking Directions:

1. Walk up the road 150 feet from the creek, crossing to a path on the left (it is possible to park at this trailhead). Descend the steep unmarked path for 100 feet. Look for the middle level of the falls on the left just below the upper level.

2. Follow the creek downstream 1 mile to the lower level, which is the more picturesque falls.

GREAT BLUE LOBELIA

Fall Creek Falls—Upper

Class:	Tiered
Height:	35 feet
Rating:	Excellent
Stream:	Fall Creek
Hike Length:	75 feet*
Hike Difficulty:	Easy
Hiking Time:	5 minutes*
USGS Quad:	Rainy Mountain
Fee:	None

*one way

Fall Creek Falls consists of three levels: upper level–35 feet; middle level–20 feet; lower level–40 feet.

This falls is located on Fall Creek Road north of Westminster, SC, in the Chattooga River watershed. The poorly maintained trail to this series of falls passes through dense growth of rhododendron, azalea, hemlock, and oak. The upper level, shown above, is easy to access. The middle level begins at the end of the upper level. The third level requires bushwhacking an additional mile downstream. Fall Creek, after plunging over the lower level of the falls, empties into the Chattooga River.

There are those who would say that the upper and middle levels are one waterfall. However, the physical structure and the 20-foot separation between the two sections make this two falls. The upper falls is also known as Andrew Ramey Falls Number One.

Driving Directions:

1. From Westminster follow US 76 West for 16.4 miles and turn right onto Chattooga Ridge Road.

2. Follow Chattooga Ridge Road for 2 miles and turn left onto Fall Creek Road (FS 722).

3. Follow Fall Creek Road for 0.3 mile to a left turn.

4. Turn left and follow FS 722 for 0.5 mile, where the road crosses over Fall Creek. Four yellow-and-black diagonally striped road signs indicate that the creek crosses under the road. Park on the roadside, where you can hear the upper level of Fall Creek Falls on the left.

Hiking Directions:

1. Walk up the road 150 feet from the creek crossing to a path on the left (it is possible to park at this trailhead) and descend the steep unmarked path for 75 feet. Look for the upper level of the falls on the left.

2. Follow the creek downstream 50 feet to the middle level and continue an additional 1 mile to the more picturesque lower level.

JEWEL WEED

Fish Hatchery Falls

Class:	Tiered
Height:	20 feet
Rating:	Fair
Stream:	Tributary of the East Fork of the Chattooga River
Hike Length:	1 mile*
Hike Difficulty:	Easy
Hiking Time:	1.5 hours*
USGS Quad:	Tamassee
Fee:	None

*one way

Located 1 mile on the East Fork Trail behind the Walhalla Fish Hatchery is Fish Hatchery Falls which flows across the East Fork Trail. This waterfall probably has no official name, but calling it Fish Hatchery Falls is appropriate because of its location. The major portion of Fish Hatchery Falls is on the right of the East Fork Trail extending upward for 20 feet. However, dense vegetation has obscured the upper section of the falls over the past several years. The lower section of the falls, approximately 10 feet, can be seen descending to the trail and around the large square stepping-stones mounted on concrete in the stream. The falls continues as a descending stream to the left of the trail past the stepping-stones.

Driving Directions:

1. From Walhalla follow SC 28 West for 8.1 miles and bear right onto SC 107 North.

2. Follow SC 107 for 11.6 miles and turn left onto the Walhalla Fish Hatchery Road.

3. Follow the Walhalla Fish Hatchery Road for 1.8 miles to the parking lot.

Hiking Directions:

1. Follow the East Fork Trail from the parking lot through the picnic area.

2. Follow the trail for 1 mile to the crossing where large square stepping-stones are cemented in the creek. The falls is to the right of the creek crossing, and the creek continues to the left.

3. The East Fork Trail continues past the falls and parallels the East Fork of the Chattooga River for 2.5 miles until it reaches the Chattooga River.

TOAD TRILLIUM

Flat Shoals

Class:	Shoal
Height:	6 feet
Rating:	Nice
Stream:	Flat Shoals River
Hike Length:	Roadside
Hike Difficulty:	N/A
Hiking Time:	N/A
USGS Quad:	Old Pickens
Fee:	None

*one way

Flat Shoals is a shallow cascade flowing under the bridge over Flat Shoals Road. The river drops six feet over a 50-foot stretch of bedrock in Flat Shoals River. A small beach and boulders along the shoreline of Flat Shoals River provide a nice recreation area suitable for wading, tubing, and fishing. This is a very popular recreation area for local residents.

Driving Directions:

1. From Walhalla follow SC 183 North 3.5 miles to the intersection with SC 11 and turn right.

2. Follow SC 11 North for 6.9 miles to Flat Shoals Road. Pass Tamassee Salem School on the right.

3. Turn right onto Flat Shoals Road and drive 2.5 miles to the bridge over Flat Shoals River.

4. Park on the roadside before the bridge.

Hiking Directions:

There is no trail associated with these shoals. It is possible to walk past a metal gate to the shoreline of Flat Shoals River on the right side of the road.

HEARTLEAF

Hidden Falls

Class:	Tiered
Height:	60 feet
Rating:	Excellent
Stream:	Tamassee Creek
Hike Length:	2.1 miles*
Hike Difficulty:	Moderate
Hiking Time:	2.5 hours*
USGS Quad:	Tamassee
Fee:	$2 per person

*one way

Hidden Falls flows over a series of exfoliated granite ledges and is best viewed after a rain for maximum water flow. The trail is well-marked with metal blazes on trees and large Park Service wooden signs at each turn of the trail. Common blue and yellow violets, tulip poplar, northern red oak, and chestnut oak dominate the trail to the falls. Much of the vegetation is reclaiming the land after a Forest Service controlled burn in 2001 eliminated the undergrowth that creates tinderbox conditions. Many small to medium-size rocks at the base of the falls across the creek provide places to sit, eat, relax, and enjoy the scenery. This is an excellent hike for all family members. This waterfall was unnamed until July 1995, when an Upstate resident, Norm Arnold, submitted the name to the U.S. Board on Geographic Names.

Driving Directions:

1. From Walhalla follow SC 28 West for 8.1 miles and bear right onto SC 107 North.

2. Follow SC 107 for 2.3 miles to the entrance of Oconee State Park on the right.

3. Turn right at the fee station and continue for 0.8 mile toward cabins 7-13 to a parking area on the right. Register at the kiosk to hike the Foothills Trail, Tamassee Knob Trail, and Hidden Falls Trail.

4. Cross the road from the parking lot. The trail begins beside the Foothills Trail sign.

Hiking Directions:

1. Hike the Foothills Trail (white blazes) for 0.4 mile, crossing Station Mountain Road (dirt road).

2. Just ahead at a T intersection, Tamassee Knob Trail turns to the right and the Foothills Trail and Hidden Falls Trail turn to the left.

3. Turn left and continue on the combined Foothills Trail/ Hidden Falls Trail. A sign indicates the left turn to Hidden Falls.

4. Hike 0.7 mile to steps that descend to an old roadbed (Old Horse Bone Road, FS 716), which is planted with clover and grass for wildlife.

5. Turn right onto the roadbed and continue 210 feet to a sign that indicates a left turn onto the trail to Hidden Falls.

6. Follow this trail for 1 mile to the base of the falls.

LAUREL

Hikers Peril

Class:	Tiered
Height:	30 feet
Rating:	Fair
Stream:	Unnamed
Hike Length:	0.5 miles*
Hike Difficulty:	Easy
Hiking Time:	15 minutes*
USGS Quad:	Cashiers
Fee:	None

*one way

This 30-foot falls was named by Ron Tagliapietra in his book, *150 South Carolina Waterfalls*. It was known to locals as Hemlock Falls, probably because of the dense forest of hemlock trees through which the water cascades over many ledges. It can be clearly seen by hikers on the Foothills Trail, which used to cross in the middle of the falls until the trail was diverted. The Foothills Trail now crosses the creek via a footbridge a few feet downstream.

Driving Directions:

1. From Walhalla follow SC 28 West for 8.1 miles and bear right onto SC 107 North.

2. Follow SC 107 for 14.1 miles and park at an unsigned picnic and parking area on the left. This parking area is 0.2 mile past SC 413 (Wigington Road), which turns to the right toward Whitewater Falls.

Hiking Directions:

1. The Foothills Trail begins on the left side of the parking area.

2. Access the Foothills Trail, which follows the East Fork of the Chattooga River.

3. Follow the trail 0.3 mile and listen for Sloan Bridge Falls on the right.

4. Continue 0.2 mile to the footbridge over the creek at Hikers Peril.

SOLOMON'S SEAL

Horse Bone Falls

Class:	Tiered
Height:	40 feet
Rating:	Excellent
Stream:	Horse Bone Branch
Hike Length:	0.6 miles*
Hike Difficulty:	Strenuous
Hiking Time:	2 hours*
USGS Quad:	Tamassee
Fee:	None

*one way

Horse Bone Falls is located on Horse Bone Branch near Oconee State Park. It is off the Hidden Falls Trail, 0.5 mile before Hidden Falls.

The water of Horse Bone Branch flows over and around large boulders in the branch. It is relatively easy to walk up the shallow branch on boulders to get a good view of the falls. About halfway up the falls, a large fallen tree obscures the upper section, but it is not too difficult to climb past it for a good view. Flat boulders afford a place to rest and set up a tripod for a photo.

The climb from the falls to the trail may be difficult, as the ground is usually moist and collapses underfoot. In many places there are no trees or bushes to hold on to in order to pull yourself up, and a rope may be helpful getting up and down the mountainside. The bushwhacking down to the falls gives the hike an overall rating of strenuous.

My thanks to Phillip B. Mayer of Salem, SC, for guiding me to this falls.

Driving Directions:

1. From Walhalla follow SC 28 West for 8.1 miles and bear right onto SC 107 North.

2. Follow SC 107 for 2.3 miles to the entrance of Oconee State Park on the right.

3. Continue 0.5 mile to Old Horse Bone Road (FS 716) on the right.

4. Turn right at the entrance to State Park Estates and take an immediate right (before the entrance gate into State Park Estates) onto the gravel road (FS 716) and follow the road 0.9 mile. Pass the barricaded road to the left that leads to the old fire lookout tower.

5. Turn right onto the very short road and park before the barricade across that road.

Hiking Directions:

1. The trail begins behind the barricade on the short road where you park.

2. Follow the old roadbed and signs for Hidden Falls Trail 0.3 mile to two trees on the left marked with pink and black surveyor's tape. If the tape is missing, look for two trees 50 feet apart with the Hidden Falls Trail blaze.

3. Turn left off the Hidden Falls Trail between these two trees onto a small overgrown trail that parallels Hidden Falls Trail for a short distance.

4. Follow this old trail for 0.25 mile.

5. At 0.2 to 0.3 mile, a valley can be seen on the left with mountain ridges beyond. Horse Bone Branch flows through this valley 550 feet below. At this point pick a spot and begin bushwhacking through the rhododendron and other bushes to the left of the trail. Bushwhack down to Horse Bone Branch, a very steep descent. Where you begin bushwhacking determines how close you come to the falls. Try to follow a course bearing slightly to the right so that you come out at a point on the branch below the falls. You may come out at the top, middle, or base of the falls. If you come out 0.1 to 0.2 mile below the falls, the walk up the branch to the falls is not difficult.

Issaqueena Falls

Class:	Fan
Height:	100 feet
Rating:	Excellent
Stream:	Cane Creek
Hike Length:	250 feet*
Hike Difficulty:	Easy
Hiking Time:	10 minutes*
USGS Quad:	Walhalla
Fee:	None

*one way

This is a very easy-to-access waterfall hike suitable for all family members. A well-maintained trail leads from the parking area to a platform for viewing and photographing the falls. A picnic area with tables is adjacent.

Issaqueena Falls is named for a legendary Indian maiden. According to the most popular version of the legend, she was a Choctaw princess in love with an English trader, Allan Francis. The Cherokee chieftain Kuruga did not approve and forced Issaqueena to renounce Francis and remain in camp at Keowee. The unhappy captive maiden learned of Kuruga's plan to kill the settlers—including Francis—at Ninety Six. She risked her life and escaped, intending to warn the colony. Furious at the betrayal, the Cherokees pursued Issaqueena to these falls where she disappeared from sight. They believed she had chosen an honorable death by leaping over the edge. However, legend has it that Issaqueena actually waited on a ledge under the falls for the Indians to leave and continued her journey. She succeeded in warning the settlement and marrying the Englishman.

Driving Directions:

1. From Walhalla follow SC 28 West for 5.5 miles and turn right through the gate onto the road to Stumphouse Tunnel Park.

2. Follow the winding road 0.4 mile to the parking and picnic area on the right.

Hiking Directions:

1. The trail begins beside a kiosk on the right (west) side of the parking area.

2. Cross two footbridges beside the kiosk.

3. Continue 250 feet on this flat, wide trail along the side of the falls to a viewing platform.

4. A short, steep trail continues to the base of the falls. However, this trail was damaged during the September 2004 storms and is recommended for experienced hikers only.

BEN GEER KEYS

LAUREL BUDS

Joney Woodall Falls

Class:	Tiered
Height:	25 feet
Rating:	Good
Stream:	Unnamed
Hike Length:	N/A
Hike Difficulty:	Strenuous
Hiking Time:	1 hour*
USGS Quad:	Whetstone
Fee:	None

*one way

Joney Woodall Falls is a tiered falls on a small unnamed stream that parallels Double Branch Road for 0.8 miles. The stream cannot be seen or heard, as it is located 200 feet below road level. The main section of the falls drops sharply for 25 feet over multiple layers of granite, after which the stream continues to descend for 50 feet before reaching a reasonably level flow and emptying into the Chauga River.

The falls is overgrown with rhododendron, laurel, azalea, and other vegetation. Little sunlight reaches the rocks and fallen trees over which the water flows, so the rocks are slippery with moss and lichens, and moss-covered fallen trees that look solid crumble underfoot because they are rotten.

Driving Directions:

1. From Westminster follow US 76 West for 13 miles to Academy Road on the left.
2. Follow Academy Road for 1.6 miles to a stop sign at Cassidy Bridge Road.
3. Turn right onto Cassidy Bridge Road and go 0.6 mile to Double Branch Road (FS 742) on the right.
4. Follow Double Branch Road for 1.5 miles to the end of the road and a wide parking area.

Hiking Directions:

There is no trail to Joney Woodall Falls, which is about 200 feet down the mountainside from the parking lot on Double Branch Road. The Chauga River can be heard from the parking area and forms a semi-circle around it. The falls are located about 0.3 mile upstream from the Chauga River. If you begin the descent on the right side of the parking lot, you may emerge below the falls closer to the Chauga and will need to bushwhack up the creek to the falls. If you park on the side of Double Branch Road about 0.5 mile before the parking lot and descend to the right side of the road, you are more likely to emerge above the falls and will need to bushwhack downstream about 0.2 mile.

BRISTLY LOCUST

King Creek Falls

Class:	Tiered
Height:	70 feet
Rating:	Excellent
Stream:	King Creek
Hike Length:	0.6 mile*
Hike Difficulty:	Easy
Hiking Time:	45 minutes*
USGS Quad:	Tamassee
Fee:	None

*one way

King Creek flows over a tiered rock face which is slanted backward, making the 70-foot drop seem much higher. Just above the pool at the bottom of the falls, the rock face forms a concave depression. The water flows around the sides of this semi-circle and through a narrow entrance into the pool below.

The trail to the falls leads through a mixture of hardwoods, rhododendron, and mountain laurel. The first 0.5 mile of the hike is easy, but the last 0.1 mile is wet and narrow and requires scrambling over slippery rocks and roots. Heuchera, bluets, early meadow rue, and yellowroot are plentiful around the falls itself.

Driving Directions:

1. From Walhalla follow SC 28 West for 8.1 miles and bear right onto SC 107 North.

2. Follow SC 107 for 10.1 miles and turn left onto Burrell's Ford Road (FS 708), paved for the first 0.3 mile. Drive 2.3 miles to the Burrell's Ford Campground parking area on the left.

Hiking Directions:

1. Follow a gravel roadbed beginning at the northwestern end of the parking area for 0.2 mile past an old manual water pump at a campsite on the right. The trail turns off to the left 50 feet past the pump before crossing the creek that runs under the road.

2. Follow this trail for 0.2 mile to a right turn.

3. Turn right and cross a wooden footbridge over King Creek.

4. Turn left after the footbridge by the north side of the creek.

5. Follow this trail 0.1 mile and turn left at a sign indicating the Foothills Trail to the right and King Creek Falls to the left.

6. Follow this trail 0.1 mile over rocks and roots and through vegetation to the restricted viewing area.

MAYAPPLE

Lee Branch Falls

Class:	Tiered
Height:	25 feet
Rating:	Good
Stream:	Lee Branch
Hike Length:	1 mile*
Hike Difficulty:	Strenuous
Hiking Time:	1 hour*
USGS Quad:	Walhalla
Fee:	None

*one way

I discovered this waterfall while searching for Jim Lee Falls and named it Lee Branch Falls for the purpose of this book. It is a secluded falls with no established trail, situated on Lee Branch upstream from Jim Lee Falls. It is one mile to the right of Ross Road and FS 724 north of Walhalla, within a hardwood forest.

This falls has two sections—a large upper section composed of a wide cliff with a recessed cave area and a lower section of randomly scattered boulders with the water flowing around and under them. During times of little rainfall, most of Lee Branch forms a sluice to the right of the rock cliff with little water falling over the main part.

The falls is almost obscured by a very large oak tree and other trees blown down during the September 2004 hurricanes. Some of the boulders making up the lower section were probably washed downstream at the same time.

This is a strenuous hike and bushwhack, but the interesting rock structure of the falls makes the effort worthwhile.

Driving Directions:

1. From Walhalla follow SC 28 West for 6.1 miles to the Mountain Top Trading Post.

2. At the Trading Post turn right onto Tunnel Road.

3. Follow Tunnel Road for 0.5 mile to Ross Road on the right.

4. Turn right onto Ross Road and follow it for 1.3 miles. Park in a small parking area on the right side of the road across from the Public Hunting Field managed by DNR.

Hiking Directions:

1. Hike due east across the Public Hunting Field to the edge of the woods.

2. Look for an old roadbed on the edge of the Hunting Field.

3. Follow the roadbed 0.5 mile until it becomes too overgrown. Move to the right of the roadbed where the vegetation is less dense and bushwhack in a northerly direction toward the falls for 0.4 mile.

4. The final 0.1 mile to the falls is a downhill slide under and through dense rhododendron and laurel growth.

5. With luck, you will arrive near the bank of Lee Branch. Listen for the sound of the falls to the left and carefully proceed upstream to the falls.

NOTE

This is another waterfall that is known to very few people—perhaps some hunters and extreme hikers have come across it. The terrain is very steep, and the lack of a trail prevents most hikers from visiting the falls. Lee Branch Falls will soon be overgrown, and the dense vegetation will prevent access.

Lee Falls

Class:	Segmented
Height:	90 feet
Rating:	Spectacular
Stream:	Tamassee Creek
Hike Length:	1.6 miles*
Hike Difficulty:	Difficult
Hiking Time:	2 hours*
USGS Quad:	Tamassee
Fee:	None

*one way

Lee Falls is considered one of the most beautiful waterfalls in the Upstate. Tamassee Creek drops 100 feet in four tiers to form the waterfall, and after heavy rain, three separate segments of water can be seen flowing over the granite in a rocky cove. Both the sides of the falls and the cliff behind it are covered with thick green moss and other vegetation.

Lee Falls lies deep within a hardwood forest. Rare local Oconee Bells and bulblet ferns grow in the moist environment.

There is no official trail to the falls, although hikers, hunters, and fishermen have established a path that can be followed. This trail is subject to frequent changes. Look for white surveyor's tape that helps mark the trail. Several small and large stream crossings are necessary. The water can be more than ankle deep and convenient stepping stones are not always available, so be prepared to get your feet wet. The constant mist from the falls makes the nearby boulders and fallen trees slick and dangerous.

Driving Directions:

1. From Walhalla follow SC 183 North 3.5 miles to the intersection with SC 11 and turn right onto SC 11 North.

2. Drive for 4.5 miles to Cheohee Valley Road on the left just before Becca's Kitchen.

3. Turn left onto Cheohee Valley Road.

4. Drive 2.1 miles and turn left onto Tamassee Knob Road.

5. Drive 0.5 mile and turn right onto Jumping Branch Road.

6. Drive 1.5 miles and turn left onto FS 715A, which is gravel. (Pass FS 715 on the left and continue 0.2 mile to FS 715A.)

7. Drive 0.6 mile to the bridge over Tamassee Creek.

8. Turn right before the bridge into a parking area. There is a barricade across the road where the trail begins.

Hiking Directions:

1. Hike north from the parking area past the barricade.

2. Continue 0.75 mile through four grassy fields (these are wildlife openings, which may be grown up with weeds from knee high to head high), crossing Tamassee Creek two times.

3. At the end of the last field, the trail enters the woods.

4. Follow the trail for 0.3 mile, crossing the creek and heading toward a larger branch of Tamassee Creek.

5. Follow the trail another 0.2 mile, following Tamassee Creek upstream to a point where the trail becomes rocky and overgrown with vegetation.

6. Follow the trail another 0.1 mile past an abandoned gold smelter (now reduced to a mound of dirt).

7. Continue another 0.25 mile uphill to the falls over boulders and fallen trees. Use extreme caution.

Licklog Falls—Lower

Class:	Tiered
Height:	50 feet
Rating:	Excellent
Stream:	Licklog Creek
Hike Length:	0.9 mile*
Hike Difficulty:	Difficult
Hiking Time:	1 hour*
USGS Quad:	Tamassee and Satolah
Fee:	None

*one way

Licklog Falls is divided into upper and lower sections. Lower Licklog Falls is a 50-foot tiered falls formed as Licklog Creek takes a final plunge into the Chattooga River. A small beach and sandbar along Licklog Creek and the Chattooga River provide an area for camping, recreation, and wading in Licklog Creek and viewing the Chattooga River.

Most of the hike to Lower Licklog Falls is easy, but the final descent to the base of the falls and the Chattooga River makes the last section difficult.

Driving Directions:

1. From Walhalla follow SC 28 West for 8.1 miles and bear right onto SC 107 North.

2. Follow SC 107 for 3.3 miles and turn left onto Village Creek Road.

3. Follow Village Creek Road for 1.7 miles and turn right onto Nicholson Ford Road (FS 775), which is gravel.

4. Follow Nicholson Ford Road for 2.2 miles to a parking area on the left.

Hiking Directions:

1. The trail begins beside the kiosk at the top of the parking lot.

2. Follow this trail 0.7 mile, passing through a primitive camping area, and cross a footbridge over Licklog Creek.

3. Pigpen Falls is on the left at the footbridge.

4. Licklog Falls (two levels) is located an additional 0.2 mile down the trail across the footbridge.

5. The upper 30-foot level is visible through dense vegetation at 0.1 mile down the trail from Pigpen Falls.

6. Follow this trail another 0.1 mile to a faint downhill path to the right through a dense rhododendron thicket. This path leads down to the junction of Licklog Creek and the Chattooga River. The lower level of Licklog Falls is not recommended for families and children, as access to the falls is off the trail down a steep grade.

MOUNTAIN LAUREL

Licklog Falls—Upper

Class:	Tiered
Height:	30 feet
Rating:	Excellent
Stream:	Licklog Creek
Hike Length:	0.8 mile*
Hike Difficulty:	Easy
Hiking Time:	1 hour*
USGS Quad:	Tamassee and Satolah
Fee:	None

*one way

Licklog Falls is divided into upper and lower sections.

The two-tiered, 30-foot high Upper Licklog Falls is located on Licklog Creek in Oconee County north of Walhalla, SC. Upper Licklog Falls drops 30 feet through a steep gorge. It is visible to the right of the Chattooga River Trail, 0.1 mile from Pigpen Falls through a dense growth of rhododendron, laurel, and hemlock trees.

Viewing the falls from the trail is easy, but access to the base of Upper Licklog Falls requires off-trail bushwhacking down a steep slope and is not recommended for the average or novice hiker. This falls shares a large camping area with Pigpen Falls.

Driving Directions:

1. From Walhalla follow SC 28 West for 8.1 miles and bear right onto SC 107 North.

2. Follow SC 107 for 3.3 miles and turn left onto Village Creek Road.

3. Follow Village Creek Road for 1.7 miles and turn right onto Nicholson Ford Road (FS 775), which is gravel.

4. Follow Nicholson Ford Road for 2.2 miles to a parking area on the left.

Hiking Directions:

1. The trail begins beside the kiosk at the top of the parking lot.

2. Follow this trail 0.7 mile, passing through a primitive camping area and cross a footbridge over Licklog Creek.

3. Pigpen Falls is on the left at the footbridge.

4. Licklog Falls (two levels) is located an additional 0.2 mile down the trail across the footbridge.

5. The upper level of the falls is visible through dense vegetation at 0.1 mile down the trail from Pigpen Falls.

6. Because of the steep wall of the gorge, attempting to reach the base of Upper Licklog Falls is not advised.

Little Brasstown Falls

Class:	Segmented
Height:	40 feet
Rating:	Excellent
Stream:	Little Brasstown Creek
Hike Length:	0.1 mile*
Hike Difficulty:	Easy
Hiking Time:	15 minutes*
USGS Quad:	Tugaloo Lake
Fee:	None

*one way

Five hundred feet upstream from the first level of Brasstown Falls is Little Brasstown Falls. Often overlooked, it gets its name from its location: 100 feet upstream of the spot where Little Brasstown Creek empties into Brasstown Creek. Here the waters of Little Brasstown Creek flow over multiple ledges of black granite. A large pool suitable for family activities is at the base of the falls.

This hike requires crossing Brasstown Creek, which can be three feet deep after heavy rains. Several fallen trees can be used for crossing.

An amazing sight awaits those who want to climb up the angler's path that runs beside the falls from its base to the top. A large flat plateau, with Little Brasstown Creek flowing through it, extends for several miles from the top of the falls. This is part of Brasstown Valley, a portion which, including the falls, was purchased by the Forest Service in 1935 for $5.00 an acre.

Driving Directions:

1. From Westminster follow US 76 West for 11.8 miles and turn left onto Brasstown Road.

2. Follow Brasstown Road for 4.1 miles (pavement ends in 2.6 miles) to FS 751.

3. Turn right onto FS 751 before a small bridge over Brasstown Creek and drive 0.5 mile to a parking area at several boulders that block the road.

Hiking Directions:

1. Follow the trail for 75 feet past the boulders at the parking area and pass under a power line.

2. In another 250 feet a primitive camping area is located to the left of the trail.

3. Walk left through the camping area to the shore of Brasstown Creek. Look for the small tributary, Little Brasstown Creek, flowing into Brasstown Creek. Little Brasstown Falls can be seen through the trees 100 feet upstream on Little Brasstown Creek.

4. Wade across Brasstown Creek at the junction of the two creeks and walk part of the way up Little Brasstown Creek, following well-established paths on either side to the base of the falls.

PINXTERFLOWER BUDS

Lohr's Falls

Class:	Tiered
Height:	55 feet
Rating:	Nice
Stream:	Tributary of Yellow Branch
Hike Length:	1.1 miles*
Hike Difficulty:	Strenuous
Hiking Time:	1.25 hours*
USGS Quad:	Whetstone
Fee:	None

*one way

Lohr's Falls is located on a tributary of Yellow Branch just above Yellow Branch Falls. It is tiered, with an additional 15 feet above the more visible, 40 foot-high lower portion. A good view of Lohr's Falls is crowded out by fallen trees and large boulders at its base. Below it the water soon joins Yellow Branch, and flows over Yellow Branch Falls.

Lohr's Falls was named by Norm Arnold. On the way back from a visit to Yellow Branch Falls, part of his hiking party, the Lohr family, followed the wrong creek, accidentally finding this attractive waterfall.

My thanks to Bernie Boyer of Rosman, NC, for guiding me to this falls.

Driving Directions:

1. From Walhalla follow SC 28 West 5.4 miles to the Yellow Branch Picnic Area.

2. Turn left into the Yellow Branch Picnic Area. Drive past a road to the right and park in the large paved parking lot.

Hiking Directions:

1. Beginning at a kiosk on the left side of the parking lot, follow the Nature Trail for 0.2 mile.

2. Turn right onto the Yellow Branch Falls Trail. Descend

some wooden steps and cross a footbridge.

3. Continue on this trail for 0.2 mile to a sharp left turn to a creek with a sign to Yellow Branch Falls. Do not cross this creek.

4. Look to the right and take an old logging road uphill to a small ridge.

5. As the road levels out and begins a right turn, look for a path to the right. Take the path, which descends slowly toward the creek and levels out.

6. Keep the creek on your left for another 0.4 mile as the path meanders around and over ridges and downed trees and crosses two small streams.

7. After 0.4 mile, the path turns right and ascends a steep bank for approximately 50 feet. At the top a large tree is lying lengthwise along the ridge. This is a good point to take a rest break.

8. Follow the path along the side of the large tree and descend the ridge to the intersection of two creeks.

9. The creek on your left is Yellow Branch, and the un-named stream on the right is the one you want to follow. The top of Yellow Branch Falls is 150 yards down-stream of Yellow Branch on the left.

10. Cross the creek to the right and work your way up-stream, staying as close to the creek on your right as you can.

11. After 50 to 60 feet the terrain flattens out and becomes a wide creek bottom with a mountain on the left and the creek on the right.

12. The creek swings north for a short distance before making a left turn to the west into the gorge where Lohr's Falls is located.

13. Stay close to the mountain on the left and bushwhack through the open woods. You will reach the stream again after 0.2 mile.

14. Cross the stream here at a small waterfall (be careful of the slippery bedrock) and work your way upstream for 0.1 mile to the base of Lohr's Falls. There is another 12- to 15-foot drop of the falls at the top which cannot be seen from the base because of the overgrowth. The upper section of the falls is very difficult to reach.

Long Creek Falls

Class:	Segmented
Height:	50 feet
Rating:	Excellent
Stream:	Long Creek
Hike Length:	1.6 miles*
Hike Difficulty:	Moderate
Hiking Time:	2 hours*
USGS Quad:	Rainy Mountain
Fee:	None

*one way

Just before Long Creek empties into the National Wild and Scenic Chattooga River, it cascades over Long Creek Falls. This 50-foot falls, easily seen by rafters and kayakers floating the river, is approximately 200 feet up Long Creek from the confluence of Long Creek and the Chattooga.

In the spring and summer the trail to Long Creek Falls is resplendent with wildflowers—violet skullcap, foamflower, and white rattlesnake plantain. Mountain laurel and rhododendron are abundant along the trail. Large boulders scattered in the creekbed and a beach area at the base of the falls along the shore of the river provide a place for rest or a picnic. It is possible to walk on the boulders into the falls and behind the cascading waters.

The trail to Long Creek Falls is not an official Forest Service trail and may not be well maintained. The trail is easy for the first 1.5 miles, but descends sharply for the final 0.1 mile to the junction of Long Creek and the Chattooga.

Driving Directions:

1. From Westminster follow US 76 West for 13.1 miles and turn left onto Damascus Church Road at Long Creek Fire Station.

2. Follow Damascus Church Road for 0.8 mile and turn right onto Battle Creek Road.

3. Follow Battle Creek Road for 1.8 miles and turn right onto Turkey Ridge Road (FS 755), which is gravel.

4. Follow Turkey Ridge Road for 2.8 miles to FS 755I on the right and park.

Hiking Directions:

1. Follow FS 755I for 0.5 mile to a fork.

2. Take the right fork. Twenty-five feet down this trail a Forest Service sign identifies this as a National Wild and Scenic River area.

3. Continue for 0.75 mile and make a 90-degree left turn onto a narrow, sharply descending trail.

4. Follow this trail 600 feet to the junction of Long Creek and the Chattooga River. Long Creek Falls will be visible on the right.

Miuka Falls—Lower

Class:	Tiered
Height:	60 feet
Rating:	Good
Stream:	West Fork of Townes Creek
Hike Length:	1.8 miles*
Hike Difficulty:	Moderate
Hiking Time:	2 hours*
USGS Quad:	Tamassee
Fee:	None

*one way

Lower Miuka Falls is a 60-foot waterfall resembling a waterslide. It is on the West Fork of Townes Creek near the Cherry Hill Recreation Area north of Walhalla, SC, on Highway 107.

The trail to the falls is the Winding Stairs Trail that first leads to Upper Miuka Falls. The number of downed trees and the trail difficulty increase after passing Upper Miuka Falls.

The lower falls is on the left side of the Winding Stairs Trail. The creek appears to have washed soil and vegetation from an outcrop of granite and established a course down the side of the mountain. Access is by bushwhacking through dense azalea, rhododendron, and mountain laurel. Be very careful descending to this falls. Because there is no drop beside the falls—the water flows almost level with the surface of the ground—it is easy to slip on the bedrock underlying the shallow soil.

Driving Directions:

1. From Walhalla follow SC 28 West for 8.1 miles and bear right onto SC 107 North.

2. Follow SC 107 for 8.5 miles and park at a pulloff on the right marked by several yellow posts. The parking area is just before the Cherry Hill Recreation Area.

Hiking Directions:

1. The hike begins with a steep ascent on Winding Stairs Trail to the right of the parking area.

2. Hike 0.2 mile to a right turn where a trail from the Cherry Hill Recreation Area enters from the left.

3. Hike 0.8 mile to where the trail makes a sharp left turn. A false dead-end trail continues straight.

4. Hike 0.2 mile to a small clearing and a right turn, passing Upper Miuka Falls.

5. Continue 0.6 mile on Winding Stairs Trail to the point where the trail makes its final major turn to the right. Do not make the right turn.

6. Listen for the sound of rushing water to the left.

7. Bushwhack 300 feet, descending from the trail toward the sound of the water.

SILVERBELLS

Miuka Falls—Upper

Class:	Tiered
Height:	75 feet
Rating:	Good
Stream:	West Fork of Townes Creek
Hike Length:	1.2 miles*
Hike Difficulty:	Moderate
Hiking Time:	1.5 hours*
USGS Quad:	Tamassee
Fee:	None

*one way

Miuka Falls is a 75-foot waterfall located on the West Fork of Townes Creek near the Cherry Hill Recreation Area north of Walhalla, SC, on Highway 107. Many downed trees on Winding Stairs Trail require hikers to climb over or crawl under logs and spreading limbs.

The falls is to the left side of Winding Stairs Trail. It ripples down a steep hillside and along a slab of granite, at times narrowing to several feet wide. Access is via a side trail through dense azalea, rhododendron, and mountain laurel, and finding an unobstructed view of the falls requires off-trail bushwhacking through thick vegetation.

Driving Directions:

1. From Walhalla follow SC 28 West for 8.1 miles and bear right onto SC 107 North.

2. Follow SC 107 for 8.5 miles and park at a pulloff on the right marked by several yellow posts. The parking area is just before the Cherry Hill Recreation Area.

Hiking Directions:

1. The hike begins with a steep ascent on Winding Stairs Trail to the right of the parking area.

2. Hike 0.2 mile to a right turn where a trail from the Cherry Hill Recreation Area enters from the left.

3. Hike 0.8 mile to a sharp left turn. A false dead-end trail continues straight.

4. Hike 0.2 mile to a small clearing and a right turn in the trail. At this point the falls can be heard and seen through the trees on the left. To view the falls, descend off the trail through the foliage to the edge of the creek. Use caution as this steep descent drops into the creek.

Oconee Bell Falls

Class:	Tiered
Height:	6 feet
Rating:	Nice
Stream:	Unnamed
Hike Length:	1 mile*
Hike Difficulty:	Easy
Hiking Time:	30 minutes*
USGS Quad:	Salem
Fee:	$2 per person

*one way

The Oconee Bells Nature Trail is located in Devils Fork State Park. The trail is a one-mile loop trail that follows an unnamed creek past two small waterfalls, a large beaver pond, and a large community of the rare Oconee Bell wildflower.

Located along the trail is a six-foot waterfall with a small, deep pool at its base. The waterfall has no official name because it is not a significant falls. I call it Oconee Bell Falls because of the many Oconee Bells that grow along the stream and the falls. The Oconee Bell blooms in late March and is a major attraction in Devils Fork State Park.

The falls is not a major destination, but simply one of the interesting sights along the Oconee Bells Nature Trail as it winds through a predominantly hardwood forest.

Benches along the well-maintained trail provide perfect spots to relax and enjoy the many sights and sounds of the forest. This is an excellent place for a family outing in the Upstate.

Driving Directions:

1. From Walhalla follow SC 11 north for 13.5 miles and turn left onto Jocassee Road.

2. Follow Jocassee Road 4 miles to the entrance of Devils Fork State Park.

3. Turn right at the entrance toward the information center and the parking lot.

4. Drive to the lower right side of the large asphalt parking lot to a kiosk and the trailhead.

Hiking Directions:

The trail begins at the lower end of the parking lot on the right. A kiosk at the trailhead is posted with information about the park and Oconee Bells Nature Trail. The trail is a one-mile loop trail that begins and ends at the kiosk. This trail is especially inspiring in early spring when the Oconee Bell and other wildflowers are in bloom.

Oconee Bell

Odell Shoals

Class:	Shoal
Height:	12 feet
Rating:	Good
Stream:	Coneross Creek
Hike Length:	200 feet*
Hike Difficulty:	Easy
Hiking Time:	5 minutes*
USGS Quad:	Walhalla
Fee:	None

*one way

Located on Coneross Creek in Oconee County, Odell Shoals is a shallow flow of water creating a 12-foot drop over a stretch of 50 feet of bedrock. The shoals and the creek are 25 to 30 feet wide.

Before it became private property, this was a favorite recreation area for children and adults. At the base of the shoals is a quiet pool suitable for wading. A gristmill operated at this location used the water-power generated by the shoals.

Driving Directions:

1. From Walhalla follow SC 28 West 2.1 miles and turn left onto Lake Jemike Road.

2. Take an immediate left onto Odell Shoals Road, which deadends at a private residential site.

3. Follow Odell Shoals Road 0.3 mile to Bruce Lane on the left.

4. Turn onto Bruce Lane (private drive), drive 0.1 mile, and park on the left side of the road.

5. The sound of the shoals can be heard on the left.

Hiking Directions:

There is no trail associated with these shoals. From Bruce Lane follow Coneross Creek 200 feet downstream. Private property must be crossed to view the shoals; be sure to obtain permission from the owner.

BLANKET FLOWER

Opossum Creek Falls

Class:	Tiered
Height:	100 feet
Rating:	Excellent
Stream:	Opossum Creek
Hike Length:	2 miles*
Hike Difficulty:	Moderate
Hiking Time:	2.75 hours*
USGS Quad:	Rainy Mountain
Fee:	None

*one way

Located on Opossum Creek in Oconee County, Opossum Creek Falls is a two-tier cascade that begins with a relatively narrow upper falls and fans out into a much wider lower section. The falls is located 0.25 mile from the confluence of Opossum Creek and the Chattooga River. With large boulders and a swiftly flowing creek at its base, it is very picturesque.

The hike to Opossum Creek Falls is mostly downhill. Hardwood hemlocks mix with white pines to create a pleasant forest scene. Along the trail are lush ferns and wildflowers such as partridgeberry. Be prepared to make the ascent on the return trip. Rockhopping across one stream is necessary near the base of the falls.

My thanks to Nick Kaufman of Anderson, SC, for guiding me to this falls.

Driving Directions:

1. From Westminster follow US 76 West for 13.1 miles and turn left onto Damascus Church Road at Long Creek Fire Station.

2. Follow Damascus Church Road for 0.8 mile and turn right onto Battle Creek Road.

3. Follow Battle Creek Road for 1.8 miles and turn right onto Turkey Ridge Road (FS 755), which is gravel.

4. Follow Turkey Ridge Road for 2.2 miles to FS 755F on the left and park.

Hiking Directions:

1. Walk 100 feet back up FS 755 to the trail on the right and follow the trail 1.75 miles to the Chattooga River.

2. At the river, turn left.

3. Continue upstream on the Opossum Creek Trail for 0.25 mile to the base of the waterfall.

PARTRIDGEBERRY

Overlook Falls

Class:	Tiered
Height:	20 feet
Rating:	Fair
Stream:	N/A
Hike Length:	Roadside
Hike Difficulty:	N/A
Hiking Time:	N/A
USGS Quad:	Reid
Fee:	None

This small, low-volume cascade is on the side of Wigington Road (SC 413), just across from the Lake Jocassee overlook—thus the name Overlook Falls. It is often unnoticed by visitors viewing the South Carolina foothills and piedmont area from the overlook. The best time to observe maximum water flow is after a period of heavy rain.

This falls is also known as Wigington Road Falls. Wigington Road connects SC 107 with SC 130 and serves as a scenic shortcut from the Sloan Bridge Picnic Area on SC 107 to Whitewater Falls on SC 130. Its formal designation is Oscar Wigington Memorial Highway, which was established in 1969 by South Carolina's State Legislature and Highway Commission to honor Mr. Wigington, a prominent resident of Salem, SC.

Driving Directions:

1. From Walhalla follow SC 28 West for 8.1 miles and bear right onto SC 107 North.

2. Follow SC 107 for 13.9 miles to Wigington Road (SC 413) on the right.

3. Turn right onto Wigington Road and drive 0.9 mile to the Lake Jocassee overlook on the right side of the road.

4. Across SC 413 from the lower end of the overlook is a low-volume trickle of water falling over the bedrock.

Hiking Directions:

This waterfall is across SC 413 from the lower area of the Lake Jocassee overlook, just before you drive back upon the highway. It is easy to miss; in dry weather there may be very little water flow. The combination of an excellent view of Lake Jocassee and this small waterfall makes this a good place to stop, rest, and enjoy the view of the lake and the surrounding mountains.

Pigpen Falls

Class:	Tiered
Height:	25 feet
Rating:	Good
Stream:	Licklog Creek
Hike Length:	0.7 mile*
Hike Difficulty:	Easy
Hiking Time:	1 hour*
USGS Quad:	Tamassee and Satolah
Fee:	None

*one way

Pigpen Falls is a double-stack falls on Licklog Creek in Oconee County north of Walhalla, SC.

This falls consists of two long, divided veils (the left much more picturesque) plunging into a sandy pool where children and adults can splash and play during the summer. A large and well-used camping area at the base of the falls makes an ideal family recreation spot. Upper and Lower Licklog Falls are within 0.2 mile down the trail.

Driving Directions:

1. From Walhalla follow SC 28 West for 8.1 miles and bear right onto SC 107 North.

2. Follow SC 107 for 3.3 miles and turn left onto Village Creek Road.

3. Follow Village Creek Road for 1.7 miles and turn right onto Nicholson Ford Road (FS 775), which is gravel.

4. Follow Nicholson Ford Road for 2.2 miles to a parking area on the left.

Hiking Directions:

1. The trail begins beside the kiosk at the top of the parking lot.

2. Follow this trail 0.7 mile, passing through a primitive camping area, to the footbridge across Licklog Creek.

3. Pigpen Falls is on the left at the footbridge.

4. Licklog Falls (two levels) is an additional 0.2 mile across the footbridge and down the trail.

CRABAPPLE

Ramsey Creek Falls

Class:	Tiered
Height:	40 feet
Rating:	Good
Stream:	Ramsey Creek
Hike Length:	Roadside
Hike Difficulty:	N/A
Hiking Time:	N/A
USGS Quad:	Holly Springs
Fee:	None

*one way

Ramsey Creek Falls is on Ramsey Creek, which empties into the Chauga River at this point, in the Chau Ram County Park. The hiking trails throughout the park, with shelters for picnicking and relaxing, make it an excellent place for a family outing or picnic. It is also home to Oconee County's longest suspension bridge.

Driving Directions:

1. From Westminster follow US 76 West for 2.5 miles and turn left at the sign for Chau Ram County Park.

2. Continue 1 mile to the parking area.

Hiking Directions:

There is no trail associated with these falls, although Chau Ram County Park has over 4 miles of hiking trails along the Chauga River.

PINXTERFLOWER BUD

Reedy Branch Falls

Class:	Tiered
Height:	30 feet
Rating:	Excellent
Stream:	Reedy Branch
Hike Length:	700 feet*
Hike Difficulty:	Easy
Hiking Time:	10 minutes*
USGS Quad:	Rainy Mountain
Fee:	None

*one way

Located in a secluded cove on the small tributary Reedy Branch, and known locally as Burson's Falls, Reedy Branch Falls drops 30 feet before the branch empties into the Chattooga River. The water flows over part of a 100-foot-wide rock ledge. The extended cliff beside the falls has bore holes, evidence of having once been a quarry. A pool at the base of the falls is suitable for wading, and an open area adjacent to the pool can be used for picnicking and relaxing. A cross has been placed beside the pool in memory of a life lost at this falls.

Driving Directions:

1. From Westminster follow US 76 West for 16 miles to Chattooga Ridge Road on the right.

2. Drive past Chattooga Ridge Road for 0.2 mile and turn left into a parking area beside a stone wall and a gate of stone pillars.

Hiking Directions:

1. Descend the old roadbed through the stone pillars for 600 feet.

2. Just before crossing over the culvert through which Reedy Branch flows, turn left off the roadbed onto the trail and follow it 100 feet to the base of the falls.

INDIAN PINK

Riley Moore Falls

Class:	Cataract
Height:	15 feet
Rating:	Good
Stream:	Chauga River
Hike Length:	1.2 miles*
Hike Difficulty:	Moderate
Hiking Time:	1 hour*
USGS Quad:	Holly Springs
Fee:	None

*one way

Riley Moore Falls is a low cataract on the Chauga River. Because of the amount and force of the water it is classified as a cataract, but its 100-foot span makes up for its lack of height. This falls is rated a Class VI whitewater rapids.

An attractive swimming and recreation site, this falls features a large natural pool and broad expanse of rocky beach. A large sandbar in the middle of the pool makes it possible to walk up to the base of the falls.

The trail to the falls winds through a forest of oaks and hemlocks with ferns and wildflowers such as daisy fleabane. The remains of an old gristmill, which once used the rushing water of the falls for power, are located at the top of the cataract.

Driving Directions:

1. From Westminster follow US 76 West for 7.3 miles and turn right onto Cobb Bridge Road.

2. Follow Cobb Bridge Road for 1.4 miles and turn left onto Spy Rock Road (FS 748, which is gravel).

3. Follow Spy Rock Road for 1.8 miles to FS 748C on the right and park on the side of the road.

Hiking Directions:

1. Follow FS 748C 0.5 mile to a barricade across the road. This road may be passable in a 4-wheel-drive vehicle.

2. Immediately after a small parking area at the barricade, turn sharply left onto the trail. Hike 0.7 mile to the falls.

PAINTED TRILLIUM

Secret Falls

Class:	Tiered
Height:	60 feet
Rating:	Excellent
Stream:	Crane Creek
Hike Length:	0.75 mile*
Hike Difficulty:	Difficult
Hiking Time:	1 hour*
USGS Quad:	Tamassee
Fee:	None

*one way

This falls is well named, and over time it will become even more concealed by trees and vegetation. Some sections that were visible a few years ago are now obscured by overgrowth. Viewing this falls requires off-trail bushwhacking through dense rhododendron, mountain laurel, and azalea. The creek banks are steep, and the vegetation extends to the edge of the water. Much damage was done at this falls during the storms of 2004, and some sections are difficult to see because of trees and debris piled up in the creek.

This waterfall cascades down a steep hillside in several tiers and continues downward along a long, narrow granite outcrop, ending in a small, deep pool at the base, where the force of the water is absorbed. The creek flowing from the pool is swift but calm and quiet.

The trail to the falls is the Winding Stairs Trail—the same trail as to Miuka Falls. This section of the trail also has many downed trees across it, which hikers must climb over or crawl under.

Driving Directions:

1. From Walhalla follow SC 28 West for 8.1 miles and bear right onto SC 107 North.

2. Follow SC 107 for 6.1 miles and turn right onto Cheohee Road (FS 710, gravel). On some maps this road is named Tamassee Road. The road is serpentine, sloping downhill all the way and looping back on itself several times.

3. Follow Cheohee Road for 3.4 miles. Park in a small area on the left before crossing the West Fork of Townes Creek or in a large area on the right after crossing the creek.

Hiking Directions:

1. The trail begins at the parking area on the left before crossing the West Fork of Townes Creek. This is the lower section of Winding Stairs Trail.

2. Hike 0.75 mile, ascending the Winding Stairs Trail. It follows the West Fork of Townes Creek upstream to the left of the creek for 0.25 mile.

3. The trail then makes several turns to the left toward Crane Creek. At 0.75 mile the sound of Crane Creek and Secret Falls can be heard on the left.

4. Shortly after hearing Secret Falls, leave the trail and descend to the left (south) 300 yards down a steep bank to the falls. There may be some orange flagging remaining where others have marked a route down to the falls. There is no other trail or indication of a route to the falls.

Shoulder Bone Falls

Class:	Tiered
Height:	40 feet
Rating:	Excellent
Stream:	Shoulder Bone Creek
Hike Length:	N/A
Hike Difficulty:	Easy
Hiking Time:	N/A
USGS Quad:	Rainy Mountain
Fee:	None

Located off Damascus Church Road in the Long Creek Community of Oconee County, Shoulder Bone Falls is a very pleasant waterfall on private property. The current property owner is restoring a cabin on the bank of Shoulder Bone Creek facing the falls.

This waterfall played a crucial role in the life of a family who lived in the old falling-down house on the private drive off Damascus Church Road. According to the current land owner, between 14 and 16 people living there depended on the falls for all their water needs. They got drinking water from the clear, clean water of Shoulder Bone Creek, and they bathed and washed their clothes on the rocks at the base of the falls.

A 1994 tornado which passed through this area nearly destroyed the existing access to the falls. The pathway to Sid's Falls (about 0.5 mile down Shoulder Bone Creek) was completely destroyed by the tornado.

Driving Directions:

1. From Westminster follow US 76 West for 13.1 miles and turn left onto Damascus Church Road at the Long Creek Volunteer Fire Station.

2. Follow Damascus Church Road for approximately 3.5 miles to a private drive before reaching FS 2616 on the right.

Hiking Directions:

There is no trail to this falls. The private driveway of 0.2 mile leads to a cabin, and the falls can be seen from there.

DEVIL'S BIT OR FAIRY WAND

Sid's Falls

Class:	Tiered
Height:	55 feet
Rating:	Excellent
Stream:	Shoulder Bone Creek
Hike Length:	1.5 miles*
Hike Difficulty:	Difficult
Hiking Time:	1 hour*
USGS Quad:	Rainy Mountain
Fee:	None

*one way

Sid's Falls is nestled in a steep ravine in the northwestern section of Sumter National Forest on Shoulder Bone Creek.

The 55-foot tiered falls is named for the late Sidney H. Ballenger, Jr., who documented most of the waterfalls in Oconee County, SC, in the 1960s. A book with his color photos is available at the Walhalla Library and the Forest Service Stumphouse Mountain Ranger Station.

The tornado which passed through this area in 1994 destroyed the existing access to Sid's Falls. A footpath was cleared through the debris, and it is now possible to reach the base of the falls by following the path, marked by pink and orange surveyor's tape. The last 200 feet before the falls is a difficult walk because of the dense vegetation, felled trees from the tornado, and steep downhill slope. Proceed with extreme caution.

My thanks to Bernie Boyer of Rosman, NC, for guiding me to this falls.

Driving Directions:

1. From Westminster follow US 76 West for 13.1 miles and turn left onto Damascus Church Road at the Long Creek Volunteer Fire Station.

2. Follow Damascus Church Road for 4.6 miles to FS 2616 on the right.

3. Park at the gate that blocks FS 2616.

Hiking Directions:

1. Walk behind the gate for 1 mile through four wildlife areas on the wide, planted Forest Service road, to the beginning of the trail at the upper end of the fourth wildlife area. The trail enters an area of young pines.

2. Follow the narrow trail marked by pink and orange surveyor's tape for 0.5 mile to the base of the falls.

COMMON RUNNING PINE OR TURKEY PINE

Sloan Bridge Falls

Class:	Tiered
Height:	25 feet
Rating:	Excellent
Stream:	East Fork of Chattooga River
Hike Length:	0.3 mile*
Hike Difficulty:	Easy
Hiking Time:	15 minutes*
USGS Quad:	Cashiers
Fee:	None

*one way

Sloan Bridge Falls is just one of several small falls on the East Fork of the Chattooga River along the Foothills Trail in upper Oconee County near the South Carolina–North Carolina border. The falls drops in three tiers varying in height from five to 25 feet.

Because of downed trees and debris deposited by the storms of September 2004 , close-up viewing of Sloan Bridge Falls is very difficult at this time.

Driving Directions:

1. From Walhalla follow SC 28 West for 8.1 miles and bear right onto SC 107 North.

2. Follow SC 107 for 14.1 miles and park at an unsigned picnic and parking area on the left. This parking area is 0.2 mile past SC 413 (Wigington Road), which turns to the right toward Whitewater Falls.

Hiking Directions:

1. The Foothills Trail begins on the left side of the parking area.

2. Follow the Foothills Trail along the East Fork of the Chattooga River.

3. Hike 0.3 mile and listen for the falls on the right. Viewing this falls requires bushwhacking through the storm damage that presently blocks access down to the shoreline of the river.

HALBERD-LEAF VIOLET

Spoonauger Falls

Class:	Fan
Height:	50 feet
Rating:	Excellent
Stream:	Spoonauger Creek
Hike Length:	0.3 mile*
Hike Difficulty:	Easy
Hiking Time:	30 minutes*
USGS Quad:	Tamassee
Fee:	None

*one way

Spoonauger Falls is situated on Spoonauger Creek, which flows into the Chattooga River and is named for the Spoonauger family who lived at the top of the falls. Set back into a hillside and surrounded by typical mountain vegetation, this 50-foot fan falls rushes over a stepped rock face in a broad sheet of rippling water. The afternoon sun highlights details of the rocks' innumerable horizontal crevices as the water cascades over them. During the daylight hours, bats can be found tucked in the crevices of the rock face. Another name for Spoonauger Falls is Rock Cliff Falls.

Driving Directions:

1. From Walhalla follow SC 28 West for 8.1 miles and bear right onto SC 107 North.

2. Follow SC 107 for 10.1 miles and turn left onto Burrell's Ford Road (FS 708, paved for the first 0.3 mile, then gravel).

3. Drive 2.5 miles to the Chattooga Trail parking area. A kiosk on the right marks the beginning of the trail.

Hiking Directions:

1. Follow the Chattooga Trail, which parallels the Chattooga River for 0.2 mile, to the crossing of Spoonauger Creek.

2. Immediately turn right at the sign that indicates Spoonauger Falls.

3. Continue upstream for 0.1 mile to the base of the falls.

PURPLE CONE FLOWER

Station Cove Falls

Class:	Fan
Height:	60 feet
Rating:	Excellent
Stream:	Station Creek
Hike Length:	0.75 mile*
Hike Difficulty:	Easy
Hiking Time:	30 minutes*
USGS Quad:	Walhalla
Fee:	None

*one way

Station Creek flows from atop Station Mountain, dropping several hundred feet into the valley below. Near Oconee Station State Historic Site, the creek flows over several layers of moss-covered rock ledges forming Station Cove Falls, a stepped 60-foot waterfall.

Pioneer naturalist William Bartram visited this area, and historians believe he camped here in 1775. In 1792, Oconee County's first European settlers built Oconee Station, a small wood and stone "blockhouse" one mile from the falls. The military fort and accompanying 1805 residence were intended to protect settlers from the Cherokee.

There is ample room for resting and picnicking on the boulders at the base of the falls, and wading areas are abundant in the cool creek. This falls is also known as Oconee Station Falls or Station Falls.

Driving Directions:

1. From Walhalla follow SC 183 North for 3.5 miles to the intersection with SC 11 and turn right onto SC 11 North.

2. Follow SC 11 for 1.9 miles to the community of Picket Post.

3. Turn left onto Oconee Station Road at 1.9 miles.

4. Follow Oconee Station Road for 2.2 miles (0.2 mile past the entrance to Oconee Station State Historic Site) to a small parking area on the left.

Hiking Directions:

1. A recently reconstructed trail begins beside the kiosk in the roadside parking area.

2. Follow the trail 0.6 mile to a wooden stile. The Oconee Connector Trail to Oconee State Park turns to the right at this point.

3. Proceed through the wooden stile for 0.15 mile to a crossing of Station Creek. Cross on rocks in the creek. The falls will be clearly visible on the right at this crossing.

4. Continue 100 feet on the trail up Station Creek to the base of the falls.

Stribling Shoals

Class:	Shoal
Height:	6 feet
Rating:	Fair
Stream:	Coneross Creek
Hike Length:	300 feet*
Hike Difficulty:	Easy
Hiking Time:	3 minutes*
USGS Quad:	Westminster
Fee:	None

*one way

Northwest of the Coneross Creek Reservoir, where the bridge on Coffee Road crosses, lies the surprisingly beautiful Stribling Shoals.

The water of the Coneross Creek flows over a 50-foot-wide stretch of bedrock. Before the access road was gated, the smooth rock was a well-known place to enjoy the cold water on a hot summer day. I spoke to a lady who remembered sliding down the rock many years ago as a child. The rock is smooth enough to slide on without using a float or tube. The shore of the creek is lined with small white sandy beaches.

The water drops into a deep blue-green pool about 50 feet wide. Then the creek narrows as it flows downstream to end in the Coneross Creek Reservoir. At one time a local Baptist Church used the waist-to-chest-deep pool to baptize people by immersion in the cold, clear water.

Driving Directions:

1. From the intersection at SC 183 in Walhalla, follow SC 28 North (West Main Street) for 0.8 mile to Maple Drive.

2. Turn left onto Maple Drive at Head's Produce Market and Convenience Store.

3. Follow Maple Drive 350 feet to a stop sign.

4. Go straight across the intersection onto Coffee Road, which continues into the Town of Westminster.

5. Follow Coffee Road for 2.7 miles to a bridge over Coneross Creek.

6. Cross the bridge and immediately turn right onto Stribling Shoals Road.

7. Go 250 feet to a dirt road on the right with a gate across it.

8. Park on the shoulder of the road on the right before the dirt road.

Hiking Directions:

Walk past the gate on the old roadbed for 300 feet to the bank of Coneross Creek and Stribling Shoals. Stribling Shoals is on private land, so you must get permission before visiting it.

Wash Branch Falls—Upper

Class:	Tier
Height:	20 feet
Rating:	Fair
Stream:	Wash Branch
Hike Length:	25 feet*
Hike Difficulty:	Easy
Hiking Time:	N/A
USGS Quad:	Tamassee
Fee:	None

*one way

Upper Wash Branch Falls is a pleasant roadside falls located in northern Oconee County 1.25 miles down Cheohee Road. This road is also known as Tamassee Road and Winding Stairs Road.

This 20-foot cascade is 25 feet downhill on the right side of the road. Wash Branch, a small stream that narrows to two feet, usually has a low stream flow. It is easy to walk in the branch, across the falls and up the falls. The best time to observe maximum water flow is after a period of heavy rain. The rocks around the falls are slippery and covered with moss, and moss-covered rotten trees lie across the base of the falls.

The sound of the falls lets you know it is there, but the view is mostly obscured by rhododendron and other vegetation. This is another waterfall that will be reclaimed by vegetation in the very near future. Upper Wash Branch Falls may not be a worthy final destination, but it is worth taking a few minutes to view and explore as you drive down Cheohee Road.

About 1.5 miles farther down Cheohee Road and 300 feet down the side of the mountain is Lower Wash Branch Falls, a beautiful 50-foot waterfall. The trek to this waterfall should be attempted only by the most experienced hikers and climbers.

Driving Directions:

1. From Walhalla follow SC 28 West for 8.1 miles and bear right onto SC 107 North.

2. Follow SC 107 for 6.1 miles and turn right onto Cheohee Road (FS 710, gravel).

3. On some maps this road is named Tamassee Road. It is also known as Winding Stairs Road.

4. Drive 1.25 miles and look for a place to park on either side of the road.

Hiking Directions:

There is no trail associated with this falls. It is located roadside and is mostly overgrown with rhododendron and other vegetation. Listen for the sound of falling water to the right at 1.25 miles on Cheohee Road (FS 710). Wash Branch and part of the falls can be seen from the road through the vegetation. Park on the roadside and walk downhill 25 feet to Wash Branch and the falls.

CRESTED DWARF IRIS

Whetstone Falls

Class:	Tiered
Height:	12 feet
Rating:	Fair
Stream:	Whetstone Creek
Hike Length:	0.7 mile*
Hike Difficulty:	Easy
Hiking Time:	30 minutes*
USGS Quad:	Satolah
Fee:	None

*one way

Whetstone Falls is a tiered falls that drops 12 feet across the 40-foot wide Whetstone Creek. The water rushes over the black granite bedrock and descends gently for 250 feet into the Chattooga River.

A camping site under large pines is used by anglers fishing along the shoreline of the Chattooga River. Walk through this camping area to Whetstone Creek and the falls. When the trail from the parking lot reaches the Chattooga River, a large white sandy beach and camping area are visible across the river on the Georgia side, where parked cars can be seen.

The Chattooga is swift but shallow at this point. With proper footwear, it would be fairly easy to wade across to the beach on the Georgia side of the river.

Driving Directions:

1. From Walhalla follow SC 28 West for 6.1 miles and turn left onto Whetstone Road just before the Mountain Top Trading Post.

2. Follow Whetstone Road 4.8 miles to a crossroads (Chattooga Ridge Road).

3. Cross Chattooga Ridge Road. Whetstone Road then becomes Earls Ford Road.

4. Follow Earls Ford Road 1.7 miles to where the pavement ends and FS 721 (gravel) begins.

5. Follow FS 721 for 1.3 miles (pass Whetstone Horse Camp on the left) to FS road 721A on the left.

6. Turn left and follow FS 721A for 1.6 miles to a large, round parking area.

Hiking Directions:

1. The trail begins beside a small kiosk on the right side of the parking area.

2. Follow the well-maintained, moderately descending trail for 0.5 mile to the Chattooga River.

3. At the Chattooga River follow an angler's path to the left that parallels the shoreline of the river downstream for 0.2 mile.

4. The path leads through a campsite to the confluence of Whetstone Creek and the Chattooga River.

5. Whetstone Falls is located 250 feet to the left up Whetstone Creek.

DEVIL'S BIT OR FAIRY WAND

Whitewater Falls—Lower

Class:	Tiered
Height:	200 feet
Rating:	Spectacular
Stream:	Whitewater River
Hike Length:	1.9 miles*
Hike Difficulty:	Moderate
Hiking Time:	2 hours*
USGS Quad:	Reid
Fee:	None

*one way

Whitewater Falls, located north of Salem, SC, on the Whitewater River, comprises two major falls and is the highest series of falls in eastern North America. It is also one of the most visited and photographed falls in the Blue Ridge Mountains. The entire Whitewater Falls chain consists of six different waterfalls along the North Carolina–South Carolina border.

The lower falls is located 0.5 mile down the Whitewater River from Upper Whitewater Falls. A 1.9-mile trail leads from the parking area at Duke Power's Bad Creek Pumped Storage Project to an observation platform at the end of a steep descent, across the valley from the lower falls.

The Whitewater Falls series plummets a total of nearly 700 feet for more than half a mile before emptying into Lake Jocassee.

Driving Directions:

1. From the junction of US 76, SC 28, and SC 130 at Seneca, turn onto SC 130 North.

2. Follow SC 130 North for 8.7 miles to the intersection with SC 183.

3. Stay on SC 130 North for another 9.3 miles to the intersection with SC 11.

4. Cross SC 11 and drive 10 miles to the entrance of Duke Energy's Bad Creek Pumped Storage Project.

5. Drive through the automatic gate and follow the signs 2 miles to the parking area for the Foothills Trail/Whitewater River.

Hiking Directions:

1. The trail begins beside a kiosk at the top of the parking lot.

2. Follow the trail 0.6 mile to two bridges crossing the Whitewater River.

3. Cross the bridges and turn right onto the trail.

4. Follow the trail until it intersects with a gravel road. Turn left onto the gravel road and proceed 600 feet, then veer right onto the final segment of the trail, which ascends for a short distance then descends 0.1 mile over rocks and roots to the viewing platform.

DOGWOOD

Woodall Shoals

Class:	Rapid
Height:	20 feet
Rating:	Good
Stream:	Chattooga River
Hike Length:	0.2 mile*
Hike Difficulty:	Easy
Hiking Time:	15 minutes*
USGS Quad:	Rainy Mountain
Fee:	None

*one way

Woodall Shoals is a high-volume flow and the only Class VI rapids on the Chattooga River. It is considered the most dangerous rapids on the river, dropping 20 feet over an 80-yard stretch of bedrock. Kayakers and rafters can be seen attempting the rapids in spring, summer, and fall.

This section of the Chattooga is known as a shoal because of the large pool with a sandy beach that waits at the base of the rapids. Water flows from the pool over sandbars and large bedrocks in the river, creating an inviting place for family recreation activities.

It is amazing to see how the power of such a violent rapid can suddenly disappear into a calm, peaceful pool and river below.

Driving Directions:

1. From Westminster follow US 76 West for 15.2 miles to Orchard Road.

2. Turn left onto Orchard Road at the Sockemdog sign.

3. Follow Orchard Road for 0.3 mile to Woodall Road (FS 757), the first gravel road to the right.

4. Turn right onto Woodall Road and drive 2.2 miles to the parking and camping area.

Hiking Directions:

1. The trailhead is to the left of the kiosk at the entrance to the parking area.

2. Follow this moderately steep, 0.2-mile trail down a rocky slope. Descend steep steps to the river's edge and a small sandy beach where water rushing over the shoals fills a cool mountain pool suitable for wading.

3. Along the river's edge a trail veers to the left for a more distant view of the shoals from the far side of the pool.

QUEEN ANNE'S LACE

Yellow Branch Falls

Class:	Fan
Height:	60 feet
Rating:	Spectacular
Stream:	Yellow Branch
Hike Length:	1.3 miles*
Hike Difficulty:	Moderate
Hiking Time:	1.5 hours*
USGS Quad:	Whetstone
Fee:	None

*one way

Yellow Branch Falls is located in the Yellow Branch Picnic Area. Several tables and a large shelter with a rock fireplace make this a very attractive and relaxing place for families to enjoy. The picnic area is located among rhododendron and mountain laurel with a small bubbling stream flowing through.

For maximum enjoyment, visit these falls after a period of rain. It's a spectacular sight with water flowing over 60 feet of multiple irregular rocky ledges. Four water crossings are necessary to view the falls. A recently constructed and well-maintained trail leads over small ridges and through groves of oak, tulip tree, pine, ash, and black gum. Low-growing ferns are abundant along the trail.

Driving Directions:

1. From Walhalla follow SC 28 West 5.4 miles to the Yellow Branch Picnic Area.

2. Turn left into the Yellow Branch Picnic Area. Drive past a road to the right and park in the large paved parking lot.

Hiking Directions:

1. Beginning at a kiosk on the left side of the parking lot, follow the Nature Trail for 0.2 mile.

2. Turn right onto the Yellow Branch Falls Trail. Descend some wooden steps and cross a footbridge.

3. Follow the Yellow Branch Falls Trail 1.1 mile to the falls.

PINK LADY SLIPPER

Waterfalls
of
Pickens County

CARRICK CREEK FALLS

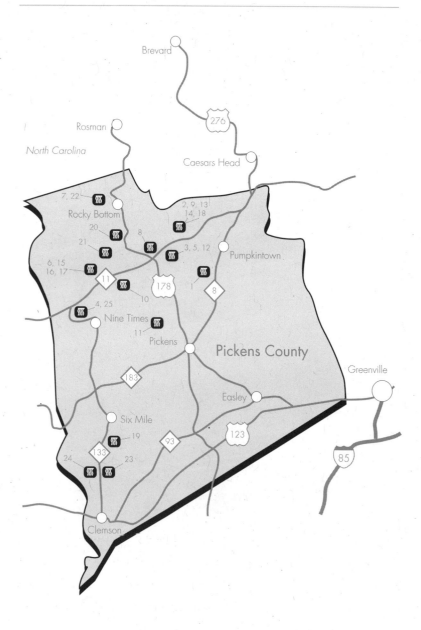

1. Adams Creek Falls
2. Carrick Creek Falls
3. Carrick Creek Road Falls
4. Clearwater Falls
5. Doe Run Falls
6. Eastatoee Cascades
7. Eastatoee Gorge Falls
8. Gauley Falls
9. Greek Creek Falls
10. Long Shoals
11. Meece Shoals
12. Mill Creek Falls—Lower
13. Mill Creek Falls—Upper
14. Pinnacle Mountain Falls
15. Poe Creek Falls—Sluice
16. Poe Creek Falls—Plunge
17. Poe Creek Falls—Tiered
18. Spring Bluff Falls
19. Todd Creek Falls
20. Triple Falls
21. Twin Falls
22. Virginia Hawkins Falls
23. Waldrop Stone Falls
24. Wildcat Creek Falls
25. Winnie Branch Falls

The upper Eastatoe Valley in Pickens County is rich with waterfalls. Experts disagree on the origin of the word Eastatoe—it may be the Cherokee word for "Valley of the Green Bird," a reference to the now extinct Carolina Parakeet, or it may mean "Green Valley of the Birds," referring to the Bird Clan of the Cherokee people, whose members frequented the area. The word itself is variously spelled with a single or double "e" at the end (Eastatoe or Eastatoee). Regardless of spelling, it is always pronounced "EAST-a-toe-ee."

JACK-IN-THE-PULPIT

Adams Creek Falls

Class:	Tiered
Height:	50 feet
Rating:	Nice
Stream:	Adams Creek
Hike Length:	N/A
Hike Difficulty:	N/A
Hiking Time:	N/A
USGS Quad:	Pickens
Fee:	None

Adams Creek Falls is located on Adams Creek, which flows alongside SC 8 about eight miles northeast of Pickens. It is 50 feet high with two tiers; the second tier is more like a waterslide. The falls can be seen from the roadside across the highway from Corn Mill Road.

Next to SC 8 on the creek side is the foundation of an old water trace that led to a grist mill. At the lower section of the falls, high up on the side of the creek, are three rock pillars, about six feet high and six feet wide on each side, which once supported the mill.

Adams Creek Falls is on private property. The owner has cleared away the vegetation that obscured the falls and maintains a trail from the upper section to the lower section of the falls.

Driving Directions:

1. From Pickens at the intersection of SC 8 and SC 183 in front of McDonalds Restaurant, follow SC 8 (Pumpkintown Road) toward Pumpkintown.

2. At 7 miles the falls is barely visible from the roadside on the right. Corn Mill Road is just past the falls on the left.

Hiking Directions:

There is no trail to this falls. It lies about 50 feet down a very steep mountainside beside a private residence. The top section of the falls can be seen through the trees looking down the creek side from SC 8. This waterfall is on private property; be sure to ask permission before going to the falls. The best viewing spot is on a curve in the road where there is no convenient place to park. Be careful if slowing down to look at the falls.

Dwarf Iris

Carrick Creek Falls

Class:	Plunge
Height:	15 feet
Rating:	Nice
Stream:	Carrick Creek
Hike Length:	0.2 mile*
Hike Difficulty:	Easy
Hiking Time:	10 minutes*
USGS Quad:	Pickens
Fee:	$2 per person

* one way

Carrick Creek Falls is a picturesque 15-foot waterfall on Carrick Creek in Table Rock State Park. It plunges into a large, deep pool suitable for wading and is easily accessible via an asphalt walkway. Several other falls and cascades can be found on the 1.9-mile Carrick Creek Nature Trail loop (green blaze) in Table Rock State Park.

Driving Directions:

1. From Pickens follow US 178 West for 8.6 miles to SC 11.

2. Turn right at the traffic signal onto SC 11 North and drive 4.1 miles to the West Gate entrance of Table Rock State Park (West Gate Road) on the left.

3. Drive 0.4 mile to the entrance of the park on the right.

4. Turn right and drive 0.7 mile to the parking lot.

Hiking Directions:

1. The asphalt trail begins behind the Carrick Creek Interpretive Center.

2. Follow the Carrick Creek Nature Trail (green blaze) to the end of the asphalt. Carrick Creek Falls is on the right.

3. This trail continues as the 1.9-mile Carrick Creek Nature Trail.

Carrick Creek Road Falls

Class:	Tiered
Height:	15 feet
Rating:	Good
Stream:	Carrick Creek
Hike Length:	N/A
Hike Difficulty:	N/A
Hiking Time:	N/A
USGS Quad:	Table Rock
Fee:	None

Carrick Creek Road Falls is another pleasant waterfall on Carrick Creek. This 15-foot tiered falls flowing over multiple ledges of granite rock is located two miles downstream from Table Rock State Park. A pleasant and tranquil stream flows from the base of the falls over sand-bars and rocks through private property.

The falls can be heard from the road, and although it appears to be far below, accessible only by climbing down the roadside slope, Carrick Creek Road descends almost to the level of the creek. Pulloffs along the side of the road can serve as observation points. However, it is possible to walk beside a gate blocking the entrance to the property and go upstream 200 feet to the falls. Be aware that the falls is on private property and No Trespassing signs are posted.

Driving Directions:

1. From Pickens follow US 178 West for 8.6 miles to SC 11.

2. Turn right at the traffic signal onto SC 11 North and drive 5.1 miles to Carrick Creek Road on the right.

3. Turn right onto Carrick Creek Road and drive 1.8 miles to a bridge over Carrick Creek.

4. The falls will be on the left 0.1 mile after crossing the bridge over Carrick Creek.

Hiking Directions:

There is no trail associated with this falls. View the falls from the roadside and respect the private property.

Clearwater Falls

Class:	Plunge
Height:	50 feet
Rating:	Excellent
Stream:	Clearwater Creek
Hike Length:	300 feet*
Hike Difficulty:	Easy
Hiking Time:	5 minutes*
USGS Quad:	Salem
Fee:	None

* one way

Beautiful Clearwater Falls plummets 50 feet onto massive boulders at its base. The two plunges of this falls at a 45-degree angle to each other make it very picturesque.

The falls is located on Clearwater Creek adjacent to the Keowee-Toxaway State Park on Scenic Highway SC 11 in upper Pickens County. It is located on private property beside a residence, and the stream flows through the property. Please respect this private property and ask permission to view the falls.

Driving Directions:

1. From Walhalla follow SC 183 North 3.5 miles to the intersection with SC 11.

2. Turn right onto SC 11 North and follow 14.8 miles to Cabin Road on the left, which is the first entrance into Keowee-Toxaway State Park.

3. Pass the entrance to the Park and continue 0.2 mile to SC 133 (Crow Creek Road)

4. Turn right onto SC 133 and continue 1.4 miles to Cedar Creek Road on the right.

5. Follow Cedar Creek Road for 0.1 mile. The falls can be seen from the roadside through the trees. The falls are not close, so bring a pair of binoculars for a closer look. The best season to view the falls is in the winter when the leaves are off the trees.

Hiking Directions:

1. This falls is on private property down the gated road that turns to the right off Cedar Creek Road at 0.2 mile. The gate is usually locked. It may be better to get a distant view of the falls from 0.1 mile up Cedar Creek Road than to disturb the property owners.

2. There is no public trail to this falls.

JACK-IN-THE-PULPIT

Doe Run Falls

Class:	Tiered
Height:	12 feet
Rating:	Good
Stream:	Unnamed
Hike Length:	100 feet*
Hike Difficulty:	Easy
Hiking Time:	10 minutes*
USGS Quad:	Table Rock
Fee:	None

* one way

Plunging 12 feet over granite ledges, Doe Run Falls is a pleasant, secluded falls in a private development and is known only to a few people.

The falls is located on an unnamed creek that flows through a residential lot. The fortunate family who owns the property has built a small trail with a wooden footbridge across the creek and made a secluded area with a bench for relaxation and reflection. The falls itself can be seen 200 feet from the deck of the private residence. Please respect this private property and ask permission to view the falls.

Driving Directions:

1. From Pickens follow US 178 West for 8.6 miles to SC 11.

2. Turn right at the traffic signal onto SC 11 North and drive 3.9 miles to Doe Run on the right.

3. Follow Doe Run 0.5 mile to Hunters Ridge on the right.

4. Follow Hunters Ridge between two ponds. Note the signs saying that there is no exit from this road and that it is a private drive.

5. Continue on Hunters Ridge until the pavement ends and the road becomes dirt and gravel.

6. The falls is located to the right of the last house on the right.

Hiking Directions:

No trail is associated with this falls. It is located on the property occupied by the last house on Hunters Ridge. Ask permission to visit the falls and respect this private property.

ROBIN'S PLANTAIN

Eastatoee Cascades

Class:	Sluice
Height:	12 feet
Rating:	Good
Stream:	Eastatoee Creek
Hike Length:	1.1 miles*
Hike Difficulty:	Difficult
Hiking Time:	45 minutes*
USGS Quad:	Sunset
Fee:	None

* one way

At Eastatoee Cascades, the usually smooth-flowing and shallow Eastatoee Creek narrows from 30 feet wide to about four feet as it is squeezed through large boulders, some the size of a small house.

Many roads and trails run throughout the DNR property along Eastatoee Creek, and there are several access areas provided by the DNR for anglers along SC 11 and Roy F. Jones Road.

Driving Directions:

1. In Clemson, at the intersection of SC 133 and US 76/ US 123/SC 28, turn right onto SC 133.
2. Follow SC 133 for 20 miles to SC 11.
3. Turn right onto SC 11 and follow it for 5.6 miles (passing Long Shoals Wayside Park at 2.1 miles) to Roy F. Jones Road on the left.
4. Turn left onto Roy F. Jones Road and follow it for 2.1 miles to where the road curves left and goes to the Cliffs Vineyard.
5. Continue straight (slightly to the right) and continue 0.2 mile (past Vineyards Fire Station) to the DNR Granny Geer Anglers Access Area.
6. Turn right into the Access Area and park in the gravel parking area.

Hiking Directions:

1. Follow the old roadbed past the metal gate for 1.1 miles to the boulder field and Eastatoee Cascades.
2. The trail follows a gravel roadbed for 0.25 mile.
3. At 0.25 mile the roadbed ends at Eastatoee Creek and becomes a narrow trail, mostly an anglers' path downstream along the meandering river.
4. Follow the path 0.5 mile to the beginning of the boulder field. The path passes behind a recently constructed house to the right up the mountainside. This house is at the beginning of the boulder field.
5. Continue working your way over and around the boulders for 0.1 mile to the Eastatoee Cascades on the left. The first 0.5 mile of the trail is easy. The remaining distance requires climbing over roots and large and small boulders. Because of this, the overall rating of the hike is difficult.

Eastatoee Gorge Falls

Class:	Sluice
Height:	25 feet
Rating:	Strenuous
Stream:	Eastatoee Creek
Hike Length:	2.5 miles*
Hike Difficulty:	Strenuous
Hiking Time:	2.5 hours*
USGS Quad:	Eastatoe Gap
Fee:	None

* one way

Eastatoee Gorge Falls is a very impressive sight. The 15-foot-wide creek is forced into a sluice three feet wide which flows between sheer rock cliffs 10 feet below the surface level. Eastatoee Creek begins its 600-foot descent before entering the gorge. The falls is located in the Eastatoee Creek Heritage Preserve, a 373-acre preserve managed by the DNR. Thanks to ideal moisture conditions in the gorge, three species of rare ferns grow here. One of these, the Tunbridge Fern, exists nowhere else in North America.

The original trail to the falls was closed in September 2004 because of major damage from Hurricane Ivan. In October 2006 a newly reconstructed trail opened which leads hikers to the Hemlock Bottoms Camp, a primitive hemlock riparian forest campsite upstream from the falls. The new trail provides a more gradual descent to the creek and the falls.

This falls is also known as The Narrows or Eastatoee Narrows.

Driving Directions:

1. From Pickens follow US 178 West for 8.6 miles to SC 11.

2. Cross SC 11 and continue 8.1 miles to a bridge at a left curve in the road. The gravel road immediately to the left past the bridge is Laurel Valley Road. Look for a sign to Laurel Valley Lodge.

3. Turn left onto Laurel Valley Road and take the immediate right fork (Horsepasture Road). Follow the gravel road uphill to the first parking area on the left at 0.2 mile.

4. Follow Horsepasture Road another 0.2 mile past the parking lot to a road and small parking area on the left. Look for a sign that says "To Eastatoee Creek Heritage Preserve."

5. Park at this entrance, but do not block the road.

Hiking Directions:

1. Follow the old roadbed past the metal barricade for 2 miles to the Hemlock Bottoms Camp, a large primitive campground beside Eastatoee Creek. The newly reconstructed trail is easy to follow.

2. Continue through the campground on the unimproved trail paralleling the creek for 0.5 mile to Eastatoee Gorge Falls on the left.

NOTE

The old Eastatoee Creek Trail is marked with yellow blazes painted on trees. Most of the blazes have faded and are hard to see. The old trail, closed and no longer maintained because the new trail is now complete, was rated strenuous because of the length and the precipitous drop for the last 0.5 mile. The newly rerouted trail is a great improvement. The announcement of the completion of the new trail was in the Fall/Winter 2006 issue of the *Jocassee Journal*, available from the South Carolina Department of Natural Resources, 153 Hopewell Road, Pendleton, SC 29670-9512.

Gauley Falls

Class:	Tiered
Height:	12 feet
Rating:	Good
Stream:	Emery Creek
Hike Length:	N/A
Hike Difficulty:	Easy
Hiking Time:	5 minutes*
USGS Quad:	Table Rock
Fee:	None

* one way

Gauley Falls is an impressive series of large boulders stretching across Emery Creek. The water glides over the boulders and continues down the creek, which empties into the Oolenoy River.

Gauley Falls is now part of The Rock at Jocassee, a gated private golf course and residential community that was formerly known as Table Rock County Club. The signature hole of this golf course is number eight. The falls cascades over 100 feet parallel to the fairway and is clearly visible from the eighth tee.

At one time Gauley Falls was accessible by an old logging road, and many Pickens County families used it for recreation. It is also known as Sliding Rock Falls.

Driving Directions:

1. From Pickens follow US 178 West for 8.6 miles to SC 11.

2. Turn right at the traffic signal onto SC 11 North and drive 0.7 mile to Sliding Rock Road on the left, which is the entrance to The Rock at Jocassee. This is a gated private golf club and residential community. Secure permission at the gate or Visitor Registration Center before continuing into the community.

3. Follow Sliding Rock Road to Whispering Falls Drive on the right.

4. Follow Whispering Falls Drive to the condominiums and park at the barricade across the road at the condominiums.

5. Walk around the barricade and up the golf cart road to the eighth tee for a view of the falls.

Hiking Directions:

There is no trail associated with this falls, but to the right of the eighth tee there is a horse trail of 0.1 mile that leads to the top of the falls. Horses cross Emery Creek at this point and descend the other side of the falls. This crossing is 30 feet from the precipice of the falls, and the creek appears to be over a foot deep with swift currents. A foot crossing by an individual is not advised.

Green Creek Falls

Class:	Tiered
Height:	20 feet
Rating:	Good
Stream:	Green Creek
Hike Length:	0.4 mile*
Hike Difficulty:	Moderate
Hiking Time:	30 minutes*
USGS Quad:	Table Rock
Fee:	$2 per person

* one way

Green Creek Falls is located on the Table Rock Trail in Table Rock State Park. This is a nice multi-tiered waterfall that cascades for 20 feet over rocky ledges before dropping into a pleasant stream that flows into Carrick Creek.

The falls can easily be seen from the Table Rock Trail. A much more impressive view is available from the bottom of the falls, but it requires working your way down a steep, slippery stream bank.

Driving Directions:

1. From Pickens follow US 178 West for 8.6 miles to SC 11.

2. Turn right at the traffic signal onto SC 11 North and drive 4.1 miles to the West Gate entrance of Table Rock State Park (West Gate Road) on the left.

3. Drive 0.4 mile to the entrance of the park on the right.

4. Turn right and drive 0.7 mile to the parking lot.

Hiking Directions:

1. The asphalt trail begins behind the Carrick Creek Interpretive Center.

2. Follow the trail to the end of the asphalt. Carrick Creek Falls is on the right.

3. Beyond Carrick Creek Falls, at 0.1 mile, bear right at the fork onto Table Rock Trail (red blaze).

4. Continue 0.3 mile and listen and look for Green Creek Falls below and to the left.

TROUT LILY

Long Shoals

Class:	Shoal
Height:	15 feet
Rating:	Good
Stream:	Little Eastatoe Creek
Hike Length:	N/A
Hike Difficulty:	N/A
Hiking Time:	N/A
USGS Quad:	Sunset
Fee:	None

Long Shoals is a newly developed recreation area (called Long Shoals Roadside Park) adjacent to SC 11. This area has been known to local citizens for many years as Sliding Rock. The shoals is located on S.C. Forestry Commission property and was abused by off-road vehicles for 30 years. The area has been reclaimed by citizens working in concert with many government and nonprofit organizations and transformed into a family recreation area. Future plans for Long Shoals Roadside Park include more trails, an observation deck, bear-proof trash cans, and an information kiosk.

The total drop of the Long Shoals is 15 feet over a 500-foot distance on Little Eastatoe Creek. On most summer days children and adults can be seen tubing or sliding down the bedrock into deep refreshing pools.

Driving Directions:

1. From Pickens follow US 178 West for 8.6 miles to SC 11.

2. Turn left at the traffic signal onto SC 11 South and drive 6.2 miles to a roadside sign for Long Shoals Roadside Park.

3. Turn left into the large gravel parking lot.

Hiking Directions:

There is no trail associated with these shoals. To view them, walk around a vehicle barrier and down a wide gravel roadbed that leads down to the shoreline of the creek.

St. Johns Wort

Meece Shoals

Class:	Shoal
Height:	15 feet
Rating:	Nice
Stream:	Twelvemile River
Hike Length:	Roadside
Hike Difficulty:	N/A
Hiking Time:	N/A
USGS Quad:	Sunset
Fee:	None

The Middle Fork of Twelvemile River flows in a northwesterly direction past the old red Meece Mill. The river is small but tumultuous here, nestled between the banks of the river and Meece Mill Road.

The waters forming the shoals flow from a concrete dam impoundment 100 yards upstream of the mill. The impoundment provided swiftly flowing water that powered the waterwheel when the gristmill was in operation over 100 years ago. The water drops over many jagged rock ledges in the river; some may call this a rapid.

Today the mill is a restaurant that serves a barbecue and hot dog lunch on the third Saturday of each month.

Driving Directions:

1. From Pickens, follow US 178 West for 6.3 miles to Meece Mill Road.

2. Turn left and continue 3.1 miles (crossing E. Preston McDaniel road at 1.7 miles) to the parking lot and mill on the left. Two areas are available for parking, one at the mill itself and the other 0.1 miles before the mill.

Hiking Directions:

There is no trail associated with these shoals, which are visible from both the roadside and the parking lot behind the mill.

RUE ANEMONE OR WINDFLOWER

Mill Creek Falls—Lower

Class:	Waterslide
Height:	50 feet
Rating:	Good
Stream:	Mill Creek
Hike Length:	0.4 mile*
Hike Difficulty:	Moderate
Hiking Time:	30 minutes*
USGS Quad:	Table Rock
Fee:	None

* one way

Mill Creek Falls is located on lower Mill Creek on Hickory Hollow Road, which turns off SC 11 before you get to Table Rock State Park. This is the same Mill Creek that flows through Table Rock State Park.

The waterfall is a steep vertical slide 50 feet high with a moderate volume of water rushing over the granite rock layers. The falls is on private property but can be heard from the roadside. As you drive down Hickory Hollow Road, at 0.7 mile you can see where the ground has been cleared by earthmoving equipment, perhaps to cover up some of the trash that has been illegally dumped into the deep ravine next to the road. If you park on the side of the road you can hear the sound of the rushing water and see the remains of discarded household garbage and vehicle tires. You'll forget all the garbage as you approach and view the beautiful waterslide and deep pool at its base. From the pool, the waters continue to meander past large boulders in Mill Creek.

My thanks to Bernie Boyer of Rosman, NC, for guiding me to this falls.

Driving Directions:

1. From Pickens follow US 178 West for 8.6 miles to SC 11.

2. Turn right at the traffic signal onto SC 11 North and drive 2.9 miles to Hickory Hollow Road on the right.

3. Turn right onto Hickory Hollow Road and go 0.7 mile to a small pulloff on the left side of the road beside a wire fence with metal posts. A trash dump will be obvious as you look past the wire fence down the mountainside.

Hiking Directions:

1. Park near the start of the wire fence and begin a downhill trek for 0.4 mile partially through the trash dump to Mill Creek at the bottom of the ravine. Try to veer a little to the left as you descend the mountain toward the sound of the falls. Because of the overgrowth, the falls will not become visible until you are very close to it. Let the sound of falling water be your guide.

2. There is no trail, so bushwhacking will be necessary the entire distance.

3. When you reach Mill Creek turn left and follow it a short distance to the base of the falls.

4. Mill Creek Falls is on private property that has been abused by the dumping of trash. Be sure to locate the owner of the property and ask permission to go to the falls.

Mill Creek Falls—Upper

Class:	Tiered
Height:	25 feet
Rating:	Good
Stream:	Mill Creek
Hike Length:	2.9 miles*
Hike Difficulty:	Moderate
Hiking Time:	2.5 hours*
USGS Quad:	Table Rock
Fee:	$2 per person

* one way

Mill Creek Falls is located on the Pinnacle Mountain Trail in Table Rock State Park. The trail crosses near the bottom of the falls. Twenty to 30 feet of the waterfall is visible by looking to the right up the falls from the trail. Another 15 feet is visible by looking left down the falls from the trail.

Mill Creek Falls is 0.7 mile up the Pinnacle Mountain Trail from Spring Bluff Falls.

Driving Directions:

1. From Pickens follow US 178 West for 8.6 miles to SC 11.

2. Turn right at the traffic signal onto SC 11 North and drive 4.1 miles to the West Gate entrance of Table Rock State Park (West Gate Road) on the left.

3. Drive 0.4 mile to the entrance of the park on the right.

4. Turn right and drive 0.7 mile to the parking lot.

Hiking Directions:

1. The asphalt trail begins behind the Carrick Creek Interpretive Center.

2. Follow the Pinnacle Mountain Trail (yellow blaze) for 2.9 miles to the base of the falls.

YELLOW HONEYSUCKLE

Pinnacle Mountain Falls

BERNIE BOYER

Class:	Tiered
Height:	100 feet
Rating:	Good
Stream:	Mill Creek
Hike Length:	1.4 miles*
Hike Difficulty:	Moderate
Hiking Time:	1.5 hours*
USGS Quad:	Table Rock
Fee:	$2 per person

* one way

Pinnacle Mountain Falls is located on the side of Pinnacle Mountain on the Wesleyan Methodist Camp property adjacent to Table Rock State Park on SC 11. The falls are at the end of a rough trail that turns off the Palmetto Trail.

This multi-tiered waterfall on Mill Creek drops 100 feet over varied rock structures. The falls begins as two tiers, but then the water flows under, over, and between boulders and beautiful rock shelves. Many large trees felled during the heavy rains resulting from Hurricanes Ivan and Frances in September 2004 clutter the base of the falls.

The Palmetto Trail and spur trail become steep and difficult near the falls, but the beauty of the falls is well worth the effort. The Palmetto Trail begins on State Park Property, but the spur trail and the falls are on private property owned by the Wesleyan Methodist Camp.

My thanks to Bernie Boyer of Rosman, NC, for the use of this photo and for guiding me to this falls.

Driving Directions:

1. From Pickens follow US 178 West for 8.6 miles to SC 11.

2. Turn right at the traffic signal onto SC 11 North and drive 4.1 miles to the West Gate entrance of Table Rock State Park (West Gate Road) on the left.

3. Drive 0.4 mile to the entrance of the park on the right.

4. Turn right and drive 0.1 mile and turn left onto the road to the Country Store on the left.

5. Drive 0.2 mile past the Country Store and through the campground to the end of the parking lot; park here.

6. The Palmetto Trail begins at a kiosk at the end of the parking lot.

Hiking Directions:

1. Begin on the Palmetto Trail at the end of the parking lot. Follow the Palmetto Trail for 0.6 mile to the intersection of an old roadbed behind some old storage buildings (or barns) on the Wesleyan Methodist Camp property.

2. Follow the old roadbed to the right for 0.4 mile (it will narrow to a trail) to a vertical marker that indicates the Palmetto Trail continues straight.

3. At the marker, turn slightly right onto a less well-defined spur trail and follow that trail uphill over rocks for 0.6 mile to the base of Pinnacle Mountain Falls. This is the most difficult part of the trail. The spur trail and the falls are on private property owned by the Wesleyan Methodist Camp.

FOAMFLOWER

Poe Creek Falls—Sluice

Class:	Sluice
Height:	5 feet
Rating:	Nice
Stream:	Poe Creek
Hike Length:	0.5 mile*
Hike Difficulty:	Easy
Hiking Time:	30 minutes*
USGS Quad:	Salem
Fee:	$2 per person

* one way

Poe Creek flows through Keowee-Toxaway State Park on SC 11 in Pickens County. Three small but impressive falls on the creek are accessible via the combined Natural Bridge Nature Trail (rust blaze) and Raven Rock Trail (blue blaze) in the Park.

Though these falls have no official name, they can be classified as a sluice, a plunge, and a tiered falls. The first, a five-foot sluice, is 0.5 mile down the Natural Bridge Trail. It is small and may be overgrown by vegetation. Listen for the sound of rapidly flowing water, and look carefully through the overgrowth for the sluice and smooth rocks around which the water flows.

Driving Directions:

1. From Walhalla follow SC 183 North 3.5 miles to the intersection of SC 11 and turn right onto SC 11 North.
2. Follow SC 11 North 14.8 miles to Cabin Road on the left, which is the first entrance into Keowee-Toxaway State Park.
3. Follow Cabin Road and park at the Meeting House on the right.

Hiking Directions:

1. The Natural Bridge Nature Trail (rust blaze) and the Raven Rock Hiking Trail (blue blaze) begin behind the Meeting House.
2. The three falls on Poe Creek are 0.5 to 0.6 mile down the combined Natural Bridge Nature Trail/Raven Rock Trail on the left.
3. The entire Natural Bridge Nature Trail is a 1.5-mile loop trail off the Raven Rock Hiking Trail with a walking time of 45 minutes.

BEN GEER KEYS

TULIP POPLAR

Poe Creek Falls—Plunge

Class:	Plunge
Height:	8 feet
Rating:	Nice
Stream:	Poe Creek
Hike Length:	0.5 mile*
Hike Difficulty:	Easy
Hiking Time:	30 minutes*
USGS Quad:	Salem
Fee:	$2 per person

* one way

Poe Creek flows through Keowee-Toxaway State Park on SC 11 in Pickens County.

The plunge of Poe Creek Falls, the second in a series of three falls, is located on Poe Creek 100 feet downstream from the sluice. This eight-foot falls begins with water flowing over a tiered segment, then makes a 90-degree turn and plunges four feet into a small pool suitable for wading.

This is another small waterfall that is becoming more overgrown each year by laurel, rhododendron, and other vegetation. Listen for the flow of water, push the vegetation out of the way, and you will be rewarded with a view of a pleasant waterfall.

Driving Directions:

1. From Walhalla follow SC 183 North 3.5 miles to the intersection of SC 11 and turn right onto SC 11 North.

2. Follow SC 11 North 14.8 miles to Cabin Road on the left, which is the first entrance into Keowee-Toxaway State Park.

3. Follow Cabin Road and park at the Meeting House on the right.

Hiking Directions:

1. The Natural Bridge Nature Trail (rust blaze) and the Raven Rock Hiking Trail (blue blaze) begin behind the Meeting House.

2. The three falls on Poe Creek are 0.5 to 0.6 mile down the combined Natural Bridge Nature Trail/Raven Rock Trail on the left.

3. The entire Natural Bridge Nature Trail is a 1.5-mile loop trail off the Raven Rock Hiking Trail with a walking time of 45 minutes.

WOOD BETONY OR LOUSEWORT

Poe Creek Falls—Tiered

Class:	Tiered
Height:	8 feet
Rating:	Nice
Stream:	Poe Creek
Hike Length:	0.7 mile*
Hike Difficulty:	Easy
Hiking Time:	30 minutes*
USGS Quad:	Salem
Fee:	$2 per person

* one way

Poe Creek flows through the Keowee-Toxaway State Park on SC 11 in Pickens County. Of the three small but impressive falls along the 1.5-mile Natural Bridge Nature Trail (rust blaze) in the Keowee-Toxaway State Park, the last is named Poe Creek Falls in one other trail/waterfall guide. It stretches about 30 feet across Poe Creek, has the most interesting rock structure of the three, and has the largest pool at the base.

The falls is 25 feet off the established trail, but Poe Creek can be seen from the trail just before it plunges over the falls. It is well worth viewing this falls before continuing along the Natural Bridge Nature Trail.

WATERFALL HIKES OF UPSTATE SOUTH CAROLINA

Driving Directions:

1. From Walhalla follow SC 183 North 3.5 miles to the intersection of SC 11 and turn right onto SC 11 North.

2. Follow SC 11 North 14.8 miles to Cabin Road on the left, which is the first entrance into Keowee-Toxaway State Park.

3. Follow Cabin Road and park at the Meeting House on the right.

Hiking Directions:

1. The Natural Bridge Nature Trail (rust blaze) and the Raven Rock Hiking Trail (blue blaze) begin behind the Meeting House.

2. Follow the combined Natural Bridge Nature Trail/Raven Rock Trail for 0.6 mile to a large wooden sign where the two trails split and Raven Rock Trail turns right.

3. Continue straight on Natural Bridge Nature Trail.

4. Cross Poe Creek on the boulders. Follow the trail with Poe Creek on the right.

5. Continue 0.1 mile after crossing Poe Creek and watch for a small, shallow creek that crosses the trail and empties into Poe Creek.

6. Cross the small creek and listen for the sound of rapidly flowing water. Look for a convenient place to descend to the right to Poe Creek and Poe Creek Falls.

7. The entire Natural Bridge Nature Trail is a 1.5-mile loop trail off the Raven Rock Hiking Trail with a walking time of 45 minutes.

Spring Bluff Falls

Class:	Plunge
Height:	20 feet
Rating:	Good
Stream:	Spring Bluff Spring
Hike Length:	2.2 miles*
Hike Difficulty:	Moderate
Hiking Time:	2 hours*
USGS Quad:	Table Rock
Fee:	$2 per person

* one way

Spring Bluff Falls is located on the Pinnacle Mountain Trail in Table Rock State Park. You can walk behind this low-volume waterfall by picking your way through the rock shelter behind the falls.

Pinnacle Mountain Trail meanders through a field of large, scattered boulders for 0.2 mile. These boulders form a bluff on the side of Pinnacle Mountain. As many as six small streams and cascades flow over and around the boulders and across the trail.

To see the maximum amount of water flow, visit Spring Bluff Falls during periods of wet weather.

Driving Directions:

1. From Pickens follow US 178 West for 8.6 miles to SC 11.

2. Turn right at the traffic signal onto SC 11 North and drive 4.1 miles to the West Gate entrance of Table Rock State Park (West Gate Road) on the left.

3. Drive 0.4 mile to the entrance of the park on the right.

4. Turn right and drive 0.7 mile to the parking lot.

Hiking Directions:

1. The asphalt trail begins behind the Carrick Creek Interpretive Center.

2. Follow the Pinnacle Mountain Trail (yellow blaze) for 2.2 miles to the base of the falls.

3. Mill Creek Falls is 0.7 mile farther up the Pinnacle Mountain Trail.

CARDINAL FLOWER

Todd Creek Falls

Class:	Block
Height:	20 feet
Rating:	Excellent
Stream:	Todd Creek
Hike Length:	0.3 mile*
Hike Difficulty:	Easy
Hiking Time:	20 minutes*
USGS Quad:	Six Mile
Fee:	None

* one way

Todd Creek Falls is a 20-foot block falls located on land owned by Clemson University and is in the Duke Energy high-tension power line right-of-way. The falls stretches across Todd Creek in multiple tiers. The creek flows under a bridge on Brookbend Road, which marks the trailhead.

At the halfway point on the trail, it is necessary to walk 50 feet along a low-lying outcrop of rock on the shoreline of the creek. Use caution on the slippery rock.

Driving Directions:

1. In Clemson, at the intersection of SC 133 and US 76/US 123/SC 28, turn right onto SC 133.

2. Follow SC 133 for 5.2 miles to Brookbend Road on the right.

3. Turn right onto Brookbend Road in front of Pleasant Hill Baptist Church.

4. Follow Brookbend Road 1.2 miles to the bridge over Todd Creek.

5. Park on the side of the road at the bridge.

Hiking Directions:

1. The trail (a fisherman's path) begins at the bridge and parallels Todd Creek downstream on the left side of the creek. The trail may be overgrown with brush.

2. Follow the trail 0.3 mile to a small fisherman's path that turns right and descends steeply 30 feet to the base of the falls.

BEN GEER KEYS

BLOODROOT

Triple Falls

Class:	Tiered
Height:	25 feet
Rating:	Good
Stream:	Reedy Cove Creek
Hike Length:	1.2 miles*
Hike Difficulty:	Moderate
Hiking Time:	1.5 hours*
USGS Quad:	Eastatoe Gap
Fee:	None

* one way

Triple Falls is a pleasant tiered falls located on Reedy Cove Creek 1.2 miles from the McCall Royal Ambassador Camp on SC 178. Here the water of Reedy Cove Creek tumbles over three major tiers and continues to drop over other tiers as it flows down the creek toward Twin Falls, approximately 1.5 miles below Triple Falls.

The narrow, unimproved trail begins at the camp with a 100-foot long rope to assist in the initial descent. After the descent several crossings of Reedy Cove Creek are necessary to follow the path of least resistance to the falls. Part of the trail lies in the space between rails of an old logging railroad. Other rails are scattered along the side of the creek, and at one point where the railroad apparently crossed the creek, the rails have been bent into a "U" shape—probably by boulders hitting against them as they were washed downstream.

This falls is something of a surprise, being about 40 feet wide, while the creek is rarely much more than 10 feet wide.

Driving Directions:

1. From Pickens follow US 178 West for 8.6 miles to SC 11.

2. Cross SC 11 and drive another 5.4 miles and turn left into the McCall Royal Ambassador Camp.

3. Park in the parking lot.

Hiking Directions:

1. The trail begins 525 feet on the right of the road to the left of the parking lot. Walk past the red gate and the sign that says "No vehicles beyond this point." A lake is to the left of the road.

2. Begin the descent on the right side of the road with the aid of the rope down the steepest part of the trail.

3. Follow the unimproved trail downstream 1.2 miles to the falls.

NOTE

1. The private Royal Ambassadors Camp is open only from mid-May through July. During that time many children, teens, and adults are active in the camp. The trail from the camp is intended for the use of the registered campers, and parking space is very limited. Permission for the general public to hike may be denied. During the rest of the year, the gate to the camp on US 178 is locked.

2. A better alternative trail, open year-round, begins at the top of Twin Falls (p. 194) and follows Reedy Cove Creek upstream 1.5 miles. This property is part of the Jocassee Gorges and is managed by the DNR. Just follow the unimproved trail that parallels the boulder-strewn Reedy Cove Creek upstream from the top of Twin Falls. The remains of the same railroad are seen along this trail. No private property is crossed using this trail.

Twin Falls

Class:	Segmented
Height:	75 feet
Rating:	Spectacular
Stream:	Reedy Cove Creek
Hike Length:	0.25 mile*
Hike Difficulty:	Easy
Hiking Time:	15 minutes*
USGS Quad:	Eastatoe Gap
Fee:	None

* one way

Twin Falls, on Reedy Cove Creek in the Eastatoe Community north of Pickens, is one of the most beautiful waterfalls in South Carolina. It is a must-see for anyone who appreciates the beauty of Creation. A large viewing deck with seating has recently been constructed. This falls is also known as Reedy Cove Falls, Rock Falls, and Eastatoe Falls.

The left and larger of the falls plunges from a height of 75 feet over a massive granite cliff, while the right side drops a short distance onto granite bedrock then slides down a 45-degree slope before rejoining the flow from the plunge. After heavy rain, a third cascade can be seen to the right of the other two falls.

This falls is located on a nature preserve, and a large sign at the entrance to the trail cautions, "No food or drink. No climbing, camping, swimming, hunting or fishing. No plant or mineral removal." An easy 0.25-mile trail leads to this impressive site.

Driving Directions:

1. From Pickens follow US 178 West for 8.6 miles to SC 11.

2. Cross SC 11 and drive another 2.5 miles to Cleo Chapman Highway at Bob's Place.

3. Turn left onto Cleo Chapman Highway and follow it 2 miles to a T intersection. Turn right onto Eastatoee Community Road, where there is a sign that says "Dead End."

4. Follow Eastatoee Community Road for 0.8 mile and turn right onto Water Falls Road, a gravel road.

5. Follow this narrowing road 0.4 mile past several private driveways to a small parking area on the left. Pass one sign on the right that says "Eastatoee Falls."

Hiking Directions:

1. The trail begins at the top of the parking lot at an old roadbed.

2. Follow the roadbed 0.25 mile to a large viewing platform across from the falls.

NOTE

1. For those who wish to climb to the top of Twin Falls, the abandoned rails used by a logging train 75 to 100 years ago are still partially in place. One of the rails can be seen lying on the side of Reedy Cove Creek about half way to the falls.

2. A trail following Reedy Cove Creek upstream for 1.5 miles from the top of Twin Falls leads to Triple Falls, described on p. 192.

Virginia Hawkins Falls

Class:	Segmented
Height:	60 feet
Rating:	Spectacular
Stream:	Laurel Fork Creek
Hike Length:	1.7 miles*
Hike Difficulty:	Moderate
Hiking Time:	2 hours*
USGS Quad:	Eastatoe Gap
Fee:	None

* one way

Virginia Hawkins Falls is located on the Foothills Trail in upper Pickens County in the Laurel Fork Heritage Preserve, which is part of the Jim Timmerman Natural Resources Area at the Jocassee Gorges and is managed by the South Carolina DNR.

This is the most segmented falls in South Carolina. Usually a minimum of four plunges of water at least 25 feet high flow over the upper rock ledge and down the sheer face of the rock cliff. The falls continues over several sections of layers of flat ledges at the base of the plunges, making the falls 60 feet high before the water levels out and continues flowing down Laurel Fork Creek.

This waterfall was known as Double Falls until December 18, 2004, when it was renamed for Virginia Hawkins, a longtime Foothills Trail Conference executive secretary.

Driving Directions:

1. From Pickens follow US 178 West for 8.6 miles to SC 11.

2. Cross SC 11 at the traffic signal and continue on US 178 for 8.1 miles to Laurel Valley Road on the left.

3. Turn left onto Laurel Valley Road and take the immediate right fork (Horsepasture Road). Follow the gravel road uphill to the right and past the first parking area on the left at 0.2 mile.

4. Continue on this uphill gravel road 3.4 miles, passing a gravel road to the right, and immediately park on the side of the road where the gravel road turns. Look for a sign on the right that indicates the trail to the Eastatoee Creek Heritage Preserve.

5. The gravel road to the right of this sign is steep uphill.

Hiking Directions:

1. Hike up this gravel road (or drive a 4-wheel vehicle, if the gate is not locked) 0.2 mile to where the Foothills Trail crosses the road.

2. Turn left onto the Foothills Trail where it crosses the gravel road.

3. At 300 feet the Foothills Trail makes a sharp right turn up a set of steps.

4. Turn right onto the Foothills Trail and go 1.5 miles to a bench on the side of the trail. (You will cross five wooden bridges with handrails on the last half of the trail as you near the falls).

5. The sound of the falls can be heard on the creek behind the bench.

6. Descend a set of 100-plus steps to the right of the bench. The falls can be seen on the left through the trees and brush.

7. At the bottom of the steps, a wooden post with a compass mounted on the top still stands on the side of the Foothills Trail.

8. Descend a short side path to the left of the post that leads to the base of the falls.

Waldrop Stone Falls

Class:	Tiered
Height:	30 feet
Rating:	Nice
Stream:	Unnamed
Hike Length:	0.3 mile*
Hike Difficulty:	Moderate
Hiking Time:	20 minutes*
USGS Quad:	Clemson
Fee:	None

* one way

A white-blazed loop trail was recently established to Waldrop Stone Falls by Scout Troop 235 of Clemson. The trail begins at the intersection of Waldrop Stone Road and Madden Bridge Road.

A large sign at the beginning of the trail diagrams the several switchbacks just before the falls and the remaining loop to the end on Waldrop Stone Road. The total distance is 0.75 mile. There is a trailside bench just where the falls comes into full view.

The stream that makes the falls begins 0.9 mile above it, flows under Waldrop Stone Road, tumbles over the falls, and continues until it empties into the Twelvemile Creek section of Hartwell Lake. The waterfall was once known as Clemson Falls, but Waldrop Stone Falls best describes its character. The water flows over and around many large boulders, continuing its descent 50 to 100 feet before leveling off in the creek.

Driving Directions:

1. In Clemson, at the intersection of SC 133 and US 76/US 123/SC 28, turn right onto SC 133.

2. Follow SC 133 for 3.3 miles to a traffic signal.

3. Turn right onto Madden Bridge Road.

4. Follow Madden Bridge Road 0.2 mile to Waldrop Stone Road on the left.

5. Turn left onto Waldrop Stone Road. Immediately to the right is a pulloff and the beginning of the trail.

6. Park at this pulloff and try not to block the gate. The gate is the entrance to one of the Clemson University Experimental Forests and a DNR Wildlife Management Area.

Hiking Directions:

1. Follow the trail (an old roadbed with white blazes on trees) behind the gate for 0.25 mile to a sign pointing to the left that indicates the falls is 0.1 mile.

2. Follow the narrow trail 0.15 mile (farther than the 0.1 mile on the sign) to the falls. Wooden steps have been installed to make hiking the trail easier.

3. The trail continues for 0.35 mile past the falls, continues to Waldrop Stone Road, and ends 0.2 mile above the beginning of the trail for a total trail distance of 0.75 mile.

PINK LADY SLIPPER

Wildcat Creek Falls

Class:	Segmented
Height:	12 feet
Rating:	Nice
Stream:	Wildcat Creek
Hike Length:	0.3 mile*
Hike Difficulty:	Moderate
Hiking Time:	20 minutes*
USGS Quad:	Six Mile
Fee:	None

* one way

Wildcat Creek Falls is a pleasant 12-foot falls in the Clemson Experimental Forest, Issaqueena Lake Area. The creek flows through the Wildcat Creek Picnic Area located on the right side of Issaqueena Lake Road. A large picnic shelter and four picnic tables nearby offer a tranquil setting for a family outing. The falls is a 0.3-mile walk up a service road from the picnic area and is a pleasant place to relax after a family picnic.

My thanks to Wayne Carroll of Mountain Rest, SC, for guiding me to this falls.

Driving Directions:

1. In Clemson, at the intersection of SC 133 and US 76/US 123/SC 28, turn right onto SC 133.

2. Follow SC 133 for 3.3 miles to a traffic signal.

3. Turn left and continue to follow SC 133 for 0.4 mile to Maw's Grocery and Old Six Mile Road on the left.

4. Turn left onto Old Six Mile Road and go 500 feet to the sign for Clemson Experimental Forest, Issaqueena Lake Area.

5. Turn right through a stone entrance and gate into the Clemson Forest. A road sign partially hidden by the trees identifies the road into the forest as Issaqueena Lake Road.

6. Drive down Issaqueena Lake Road for 2 miles to the Wildcat Creek Picnic Area on the right.

7. After entering at the gate, drive past Indian Creek Hiking Trails Recreation Area on the left at 0.4 mile, across a shallow stream flowing over the road at 0.7 mile, and past the Willow Springs Picnic Area on the right at 1.1 miles.

8. At 2 miles, turn right into the Wildcat Creek Picnic Area and park.

Hiking Directions:

1. Cross a 24-foot wooden footbridge over Wildcat Creek located across the parking area from the picnic shelter.

2. Follow the trail 80 feet past two outhouses within sight of the bridge.

3. Turn right onto the dirt and gravel service road just past the outhouses.

4. Follow the service road uphill 0.3 mile to the falls on the left side of the road.

NOTE

As the sign on the gate states, the Clemson Experimental Forest is closed from November to March 15.

Winnie Branch Falls

Class:	Tiered
Height:	12 feet
Rating:	Nice
Stream:	Winnie Branch
Hike Length:	0.6 mile*
Hike Difficulty:	Moderate
Hiking Time:	30 minutes*
USGS Quad:	Sunset
Fee:	None

* one way

This falls on Winnie Branch is probably unnamed by the hunters who frequent this DNR Wildlife Management Area. The water slides over the lower side of the large granite rock stretching across the creek. During times of heavy rain, the water covers the rock's entire surface and fills the narrow rock-lined gorge leading from the base of the falls. When the water level is low, the moss-covered rocks that line the six-foot-deep gorge leading from the waterfall are a beautiful sight. The large stone structure of the falls itself, and another large boulder beside the falls that appears to have been cut smooth with a saw, is sufficient incentive to make this short hike.

Driving Directions:

1. From the intersection of SC 133 and SC 11, turn right and continue 1.1 miles on SC 11 to a dirt road on the right.

2. Turn right onto the dirt road and immediately into a small parking space.

Hiking Directions:

1. Follow the service road behind the gate for 0.6 mile.

2. Stay on the service road, although three other service roads turn to the right. Do not make any right turns off the "main" road even if the other roads are newer and more tempting to explore. The "main" road will either go straight or slightly to the left at each of the roads to the right.

3. At 0.4 mile a beaver swamp and wetlands lie along the right side of the road. Many trees cut by beavers will be evident.

4. After passing the beaver swamp look to the right for a 10-foot high-rock outcrop at road level, which is mostly hidden by trees and brush. Listen for the sound of flowing water to the right.

5. Walk behind and above the rock outcrop on the road.

6. Make a right turn off the road just past the rock (to the left of the rock).

7. Bushwhack 300 feet down the mountainside to the creek and the falls.

LITTLE BROWN JUGS

Waterfalls
of
Greenville County

SWEET THING ON SLICKUM

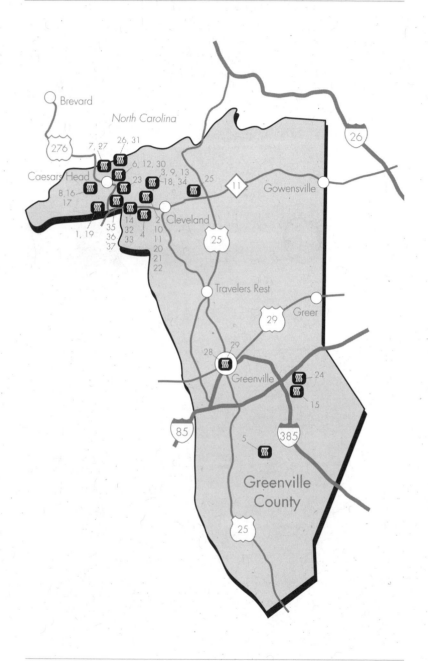

Brevard

North Carolina

276

Caesars Head

7, 27   26, 31
6, 12, 30
3, 9, 13
8,16   23   18, 34   25
17

1, 19   35   14   2
         36   32   10   Cleveland
         37   33   4   11
                    20
                    21
                    22

11   Gowensville

26

25

Travelers Rest

29   Greer

28   29
Greenville   24
            15

85   385
    5

25

Greenville
County

25

Firewater Falls. Mashbox Falls. Moonshine Falls These names give us a clue to some of the history surrounding waterfalls in Greenville County. Both falls have the ruins of moonshine stills nearby, remnants of the days when resourceful mountaineers managed to keep their families fed in remote locations where cash was hard to come by. Some, like Drip Rock Falls and Misty Cavern Falls, are most spectacular in winter, when falling water forms large icicles and under very cold conditions coats an entire cavern in ice. Whether most interesting for its natural history or the part it plays in human history, every waterfall is unique and worth seeing for its own special qualities.

BEN GEER KEYS

WILD COLUMBINE

Asbury Cascades

Class:	Tiered
Height:	15 feet
Rating:	Fair
Stream:	Tributary of Matthews Creek
Hike Length:	1.3 miles*
Hike Difficulty:	Moderate
Hiking Time:	1.5 hours*
USGS Quad:	Table Rock
Fee:	None

* one way

This hike takes you to a pleasant stretch of the creek where there is a small waterfall and pool. Asbury Cascades is located along the Asbury Trail, before reaching the cable crossing over Matthews Creek on the way to Moonshine Falls. Here the stream drops 15 feet in 200 feet as it flows over several small drops and tiers of rocks.

A marker on the side of the trail indicates a campsite to the right beside the stream at 1.25 miles. The major portion of the cascades is 100 feet up the trail past the campsite marker.

The trails at the Asbury Hills Camp and Retreat Center are open to the public. However, when the camp is in session from June 1 to the end of the first week in August it is very crowded with young people and adults. During this period, please call the camp to find out if it is convenient to access the trails (see Appendix A for contact information).

Driving Directions:

1. From the Post Office in Cleveland, follow US 276 West/SC 11 South 5.1 miles to where US 276 West turns right toward Caesars Head State Park.

2. Follow US 276 West for 1.7 miles to Asbury Hills Camp and Retreat Center.

3. Turn left onto Lakemont Road at the entrance to Asbury Hills Camp.

4. Immediately turn right and follow the road to a gate. Pass through the gate and continue 0.3 mile to the trailhead. This gate is locked at 5 pm.

5. Turn left just past the trailhead and park in the spaces on the left.

Hiking Directions:

1. Follow Asbury Trail for 1.3 miles to a wooden post marker with the cascades symbol—three horizontal wavy lines—carved into the top.

2. Turn right and follow the short descending trail to the side of the creek and the cascades.

WHITE WILD INDIGO

Ashmore Falls

Class:	Horsetail
Height:	150 feet
Rating:	Excellent
Stream:	Wattacoo Creek
Hike Length:	0.4 mile*
Hike Difficulty:	Moderate
Hiking Time:	30 minutes*
USGS Quad:	Cleveland
Fee:	None

* one way

Ashmore Falls is in the 560-acre Ashmore Heritage Preserve, part of the Mountain Bridge Wilderness Area in northern Greenville County. According to the South Carolina Department of Natural Resources, the preserve provides habitat for rare plant species, including Indian paintbrush and grass of Parnassus, and for rare animals, including the green salamander.

Ashmore Falls itself is 150 feet high, beginning 300 feet above Lake Wattacoo and sliding into Wattacoo Creek, which is impounded by an earthen dam to create the three-acre lake. When the lake is calm, the waterfall is reflected in its mirrorlike surface, and in autumn, the multi-colored hardwood foliage on the surrounding mountains presents a spectacular color mosaic. This waterfall is most visible in the spring and after heavy rains.

The trail over the dam loops around Lake Wattacoo and joins the original trail back to Persimmon Ridge Road for a total distance of 0.8 mile.

Driving Directions:

1. From the Post Office in Cleveland, follow US 276 West/SC 11 South toward Caesars Head State Park for 3.2 miles to Persimmon Ridge Road on the right.

2. Follow Persimmon Ridge Road for 0.8 mile (paved for 0.3 mile, then gravel) to a parking area on the right, across from a private driveway on the left.

Hiking Directions:

1. Follow Persimmon Ridge Road (gravel) uphill for 200 feet to the trailhead on the right. The sign for the Ashmore Heritage Preserve is at the trailhead.

2. Follow the gravel road downhill and cross the shallow West Fork Creek.

3. Bear right, ignoring the trail to the left.

4. Continue uphill, then right onto broken pavement to an intersection at the top of a hill. Stay on the broken pavement as it turns steeply downhill to the left at the next intersection. This leads to the dam of Lake Wattacoo opposite the waterfall.

5. The trail continues around Lake Wattacoo and intersects the trail to the left mentioned in #3 above. This completes the loop trail around the lake. Turn right and follow the trail across the shallow creek mentioned in #2 above and continue to the entrance of the preserve.

Mountain Sweet Pitcher Plant

Ben's Sluice

Class:	Sluice
Height:	8 feet
Rating:	Nice
Stream:	Middle Saluda River
Hike Length:	1.5 miles*
Hike Difficulty:	Moderate
Hiking Time:	2 hours*
USGS Quad:	Cleveland
Fee:	$2 per person

* one way

The major section of Ben's Sluice is downstream from this upper, easy-to-access section. The complete sluice is approximately 0.1 mile long, and its thunderous torrent can be heard after passing Campsite 11 in Jones Gap State Park. Portions of the sluice can be seen through the trees and down the gorge through which it flows, to the left of the Jones Gap Trail.

A pleasant hike on the well-maintained Jones Gap Trail #1 leads to Ben's Sluice, located 0.4 mile past Jones Gap Falls. The hike follows the boulder-strewn Middle Saluda River most of the way. This pleasant rushing stream is visible along most of the trail. A spur trail just past Campsite 11 leads directly to Jones Gap Falls. Continuing on Jones Gap Trail #1 for another 0.4 mile leads to Ben's Sluice near Campsite 12.

Driving Directions:

1. From the Post Office in Cleveland, drive 1.1 miles on US 276 West/SC 11 South and turn right at the F-Mart convenience store onto River Falls Road.

2. Follow River Falls Road for 5.4 miles to the entrance of Jones Gap State Park and park in the parking lot on the right.

Hiking Directions:

1. Follow Jones Gap Trail #1 (blue blaze) for 0.9 mile upstream along the Middle Saluda River to the John Reid Clonts Memorial Bridge, a wooden footbridge.

2. Cross the Middle Saluda River on the footbridge and continue 0.1 mile to Camp-site 11.

3. At the signpost indicating Jones Gap Falls, bear left, following Jones Gap Trail #1 another 0.4 mile to Ben's' Sluice. Look for a trail (wash) on the left leading down to a beach and pool at the base of a small cascade and sluice over bedrock in the stream. This is the upper section of Ben's Sluice.

Blythe Shoals

Class:	Shoal
Height:	15 feet
Rating:	Nice
Stream:	South Saluda River
Hike Length:	Roadside
Hike Difficulty:	N/A
Hiking Time:	N/A
USGS Quad:	Cleveland
Fee:	None

Blythe Shoals is a Class III-IV rapids 0.5 mile off scenic SC 11 in upper Greenville County. It can easily be viewed from South Blythe Shoals Road. The rapids flows over a large outcrop of rock on the South Saluda River, with a total drop of 15 to 20 feet over a half-mile downstream run. The Saluda River forms the border between Greenville, Pickens, and Anderson Counties.

Blythe Shoals is a very dangerous rapids, and many accidents and injuries have occurred when people tried to wade and tube there. Because of this, the roadside is heavily posted with No Trespassing signs.

Driving Directions:

1. From the Post Office in Cleveland, follow US 276 West/SC 11 for 2.9 miles, passing Blythe Shoals Produce on the right.

2. Continue 0.1 mile to South Blythe Shoals Road on the left.

3. Turn left onto South Blythe Shoals Road and continue 0.5 mile until the shoals become visible on the right side of the road. The roadside is well posted with No Trespassing signs. View the shoals from the roadside without violating the private property.

Hiking Directions:

There is no trail associated with these shoals. Use caution while viewing them as they are about 20 feet below road level.

WILD STRAWBERRY

Cedar Shoals

Class:	Block
Height:	12 feet
Rating:	Excellent
Stream:	Reedy River
Hike Length:	Roadside
Hike Difficulty:	Easy
Hiking Time:	N/A
USGS Quad:	Fork Shoals
Fee:	None

Reedy River, which flows through the City of Greenville, reaches southern Greenville County at Cedar Shoals. A 20-foot-high masonry dam partway across the river creates a 50-foot-wide block waterfall. On the other part of the river is a 50-foot-wide shoals that drops 12 feet. The dam was probably built to provide waterpower to a gristmill or sawmill.

A large field with sandy areas is at the access point to this falls. There is much evidence of fishing activity along the shoreline of Reedy River as it passes under Cedar Falls Road. Many temporary anglers' campsites litter the way to the falls, even though this is private property.

Driving Directions:

1. From Greenville, drive south on I-385 to exit 27.

2. Turn right onto Fairview Road and drive 3.9 miles to the intersection with SC 418.

3. Turn right onto SC 418 and continue 2.5 miles to Fork Shoals Road.

4. Turn left onto Fork Shoals Road and follow it for 1.7 miles to McKelvey Road.

5. Turn right onto McKelvey Road.

6. Drive 0.3 mile and turn left onto Cedar Falls Road.

7. Drive 0.8 mile, at which point the road curves to the right with a small pulloff on the left. Park there, before the bridge on Cedar Falls Road.

Hiking Directions:

There is no trail associated with this falls. The shoals are visible from the roadside, and the falls requires a 300-foot walk upstream. From the small parking area, follow a dirt road blocked by fallen trees that leads down into an open field and then to the river.

Cliff Falls

Class:	Tiered
Height:	20 feet
Rating:	Good
Stream:	Cliff Creek
Hike Length:	0.8 mile*
Hike Difficulty:	Moderate
Hiking Time:	1 hour*
USGS Quad:	Cleveland
Fee:	$2 per person

* one way

Cliff Falls flows over multiple ledges of granite as it tumbles 20 feet down the side of a mountain on Cliff Creek in Caesars Head State Park. Frank Coggins Trail #15 leads to a narrow footbridge at the top of the falls. For a better view, it is necessary to follow Rim of The Gap Trail #6 for 100 feet, then turn left onto a steep path that leads to the rocky edges of the falls.

Cliff Falls, Firewater Falls, and Rockcliff Falls are all accessible along Frank Coggins Trail #15 at Caesars Head State Park.

Driving Directions:

1. From the Post Office in Cleveland follow US 276 West/ SC 11 South for 5.1 miles, where US 276 turns right and SC 11 continues straight.

2. Turn right, staying on US 276, and continue 7.4 miles to Caesars Head State Park and the visitors center.

3. Park at the visitors center and cross US 276 to the trailhead.

Hiking Directions:

1. Follow Frank Coggins Trail #15 (purple blaze) 0.8 mile to a footbridge at the top of Cliff Falls.

2. At this point, Frank Coggins Trail #15 connects with Rim of The Gap Trail #6 (yellow blaze) and Naturaland Trust Trail #14 (pink blaze).

3. Turn left onto Rim of The Gap Trail #6 and hike 100 feet to a steep, short side trail to the left.

4. Turn left onto this side trail to view the upper tiers of Cliff Falls.

MAYAPPLE

Dargans Cascade

Class:	Block
Height:	25 feet
Rating:	Good
Stream:	Middle Saluda River
Hike Length:	1.2 miles*
Hike Difficulty:	Strenuous
Hiking Time:	1 hour*
USGS Quad:	Cleveland
Fee:	$2 per person

* one way

Dargans Cascade, located beside the Jones Gap Trail, consists of two sections. Both the upper block falls and the lower section can be seen from the trail. The upper section is visible as you cross the Middle Saluda River on the fallen tree at the top of the falls. The lower section begins just past a small sandy beach at the base of the upper section.

The upper section, where water flows over a 15-foot drop of slick granite bedrock, is similar to a waterslide. The lower section, formed by water forced between and around randomly scattered, moss-covered boulders, can be seen through the trees and undergrowth from Jones Gap Trail. A curve in the river and much debris and vegetation prevents a good view of both sections at the same time.

Driving Directions:

1. From the Post Office in Cleveland follow US 276 West/SC 11 South for 5.1 miles to where US 276 turns right and SC 11 continues straight.

2. Turn right, staying on US 276, and continue 7.4 miles to Caesars Head State Park and the visitors center.

3. Follow US 276 west past Caesars Head State Park for 1.1 miles and turn right into the parking area designated for Raven Cliff Parking.

Hiking Directions:

1. Tom Miller Trail #2 (blue blaze) begins near the entrance of the Raven Cliff parking lot.

2. Follow Tom Miller Trail downhill 0.7 mile to the intersection of Jones Gap Trail #1 (blue blaze). This trail is rated strenuous and drops from 2,920 feet to 2,560 feet over 0.7 mile. The trek down requires strong knees, and the climb up requires strong legs, lungs, and cardiovascular system.

3. At the intersection with Jones Gap Trail, turn right and continue 0.5 mile to the log crossing over the Middle Saluda River and Dargans Cascade.

4. Reaching the base of Dargans Cascade requires a short bushwhack off the trail to the right, down the side of the falls.

DOGHOBBLE

Drip Rock Falls

Class:	Plunge
Height:	12 feet
Rating:	Nice
Stream:	Oil Camp Creek
Hike Length:	Roadside
Hike Difficulty:	N/A
Hiking Time:	N/A
USGS Quad:	Cleveland
Fee:	None

Drip Rock Falls may be significant only because its waters are the headwaters of Oil Camp Creek. This plunge of slowly flowing water produces spectacularly large icicles in the winter. In freezing weather, large sheets of ice form over the bedrock; the entire cavern can be coated with ice.

The falls is located on US 276 West 5.2 miles from the intersection with SC 11, two miles before Caesars Head State Park. To spot this falls and cavern, you must be looking to the left side of the road as you go around one of the many curves before arriving at Caesars Head State Park.

Driving Directions:

1. From the Post Office in Cleveland follow US 276 West/ SC 11 South for 5.1 miles to where US 276 turns right and SC 11 continues straight.

2. Turn right, staying on US 276, and continue 5.2 miles to Drip Rock Falls on the left.

3. Pull off to the right onto a small roadside parking space across from the falls.

Hiking Directions:

There is no trail associated with this falls; it is visible from the roadside. Use caution: the falls and small parking space are on a curve in the road.

WITCH ALDER

Eastern Stream Falls

Class:	Tiered
Height:	50 feet
Rating:	Nice
Stream:	Eastern Stream
Hike Length:	1.1 miles*
Hike Difficulty:	Moderate
Hiking Time:	1.5 hours*
USGS Quad:	Cleveland
Fee:	None

* one way

Eastern Stream Falls is a cataract bog created by a low-volume stream flowing across a steep rock face.

A cataract bog is an open seepage area on a granite exposure. It forms where a permanent stream flows slowly over a steeply sloped rock outcrop. At the edges of the stream, a thin layer of soil with a spongy area of decomposing vegetation supports rare plant species such as yellow painted cup, grass of Parnassus, mountain sweet pitcher plant, and other moisture-loving plants.

Visit this falls after heavy rains for maximum water flow.

Driving Directions:

1. From the Post Office in Cleveland, drive 1.1 miles on US 276 West/SC 11 South and turn right at the F-Mart convenience store onto River Falls Road.

2. Follow River Falls Road for 2.9 miles to Oil Camp Creek Road on the left.

3. Turn left onto Oil Camp Creek Road and drive 1.9 miles to where the pavement ends.

4. Follow the dirt road 0.1 mile to a small parking area.

Hiking Directions:

1. Walk around a green metal barricade and hike 0.5 mile to another metal barricade painted red.

2. Walk around this barricade and continue 250 feet to Pinnacle Pass Trail #20 (orange blaze) on the right.

3. Follow Pinnacle Pass Trail #20 steeply uphill for 0.6 mile to the base of the falls. The falls are on the right side of the trail.

4. Eastern Stream Falls divides into three sections as it flows around boulders and across Pinnacle Pass Trail at three locations. The first two crossings of the trail require some walking across rocks.

5. The third and most difficult crossing has a cable across the stream to help prevent slipping on the rocks at the base of the falls.

Oblong Leaved Sundew

Emerald Falls

Class:	Tiered
Height:	15 feet
Rating:	Fair
Stream:	Unnamed
Hike Length:	0.1 mile*
Hike Difficulty:	Easy
Hiking Time:	10 minutes*
USGS Quad:	Cleveland
Fee:	None

* one way

Emerald Falls is a secluded 15-foot falls located on a shallow stream that meanders through a private development along SC 11 in upper Greenville County. At the upper level of the falls, a small, attractive wooden bridge has been built across the stream, which has become overgrown in the past few years.

Occasionally someone representing a real estate agency is available at one of the office buildings on the right after the entrance on Copperline Drive. If so, ask for directions and permission to hike to the falls.

Driving Directions:

1. From the Post Office in Cleveland, follow US 276 West/ SC 11 South for 2.4 miles to the entrance to Emerald Falls Subdivision.

2. Turn right into the entrance, on Copperline Drive.

3. This is private property and the developer has posted a sign indicating that neither a road nor a trail is available to the falls.

Hiking Directions:

Since there is no established trail to this falls, visitation is discouraged. Some lots adjacent to the falls are available for sale, and some lots have a view of the falls.

JACK-IN-THE-PULPIT

Falls Creek Falls

Class:	Tiered
Height:	125 feet
Rating:	Excellent
Stream:	Falls Creek
Hike Length:	1.2 miles*
Hike Difficulty:	Strenuous
Hiking Time:	2 hours*
USGS Quad:	Standingstone Mountain
Fee:	None

* one way

Do not confuse Falls Creek Falls with Fall Creek Falls located near Westminster, SC. This falls, at 125 feet high, is much more impressive than Fall Creek Falls.

Every waterfall is unique, but this one has more large flat ledges than almost any other, and its different sections—plunge, slide, block, and fan—create a pleasingly complex structure. The refreshing sight of the water flowing over these ledges makes the strenuous hike worthwhile.

This strenuous hike is a steep uphill grade, with only a few short level areas, all the way to the falls. The trail ascends approximately 600 feet over the 1.2 mile distance.

Driving Directions:

1. From the Post Office in Cleveland, drive 1.1 miles on US 276 West/SC 11 South and turn right at the F-Mart convenience store onto River Falls Road.

2. Follow River Falls Road for 4 miles and turn right onto Duckworth Road. Look for the Palmetto Bible Camp sign.

3. Follow Duckworth Road for 0.5 mile and turn right onto Fall Creek Road. Watch for a second Palmetto Bible Camp sign.

4. Follow Fall Creek Road for 0.4 mile, passing the Palmetto Bible Camp on the right.

5. Cross a small bridge and park at the parking area on the left.

Hiking Directions:

1. From the trailhead at the kiosk in the parking area, follow Falls Creek Trail #31 (orange blaze) uphill. A water crossing over Little Falls Creek at 0.7 mile requires some rockhopping.

2. Continue on the trail through a field of large granite boulders.

3. Descend to a steep crossing over Falls Creek for a view of the falls. Three lengths of cable provide handholds during the descent across the rocks at the bottom of the falls.

4. The trail continues as Hospital Rock Trail #30 (orange blaze) beyond the falls and terminates in Jones Gap State Park.

Ox-eye Daisy

Firewater Falls

Class:	Plunge
Height:	20 feet
Rating:	Fair
Stream:	Cliff Creek
Hike Length:	1.1 miles*
Hike Difficulty:	Moderate
Hiking Time:	1.5 hours*
USGS Quad:	Cleveland
Fee:	$2 per person

* one way

Located trailside on the Naturaland Trust Trail in Caesars Head State Park, Firewater Falls' impressive low-volume flow plunges 20 feet from the top of a cliff and past the cavern behind it, splashing into Cliff Creek at its base. The black granite shelf which creates the waterfall is 100 feet wide.

The name of the falls derives from remains of an old moonshine still that once sat atop the granite shelf. Archaeologists have found some evidence that Indians frequently used the cave at the base of the cliff for shelter.

Cliff Falls, Firewater Falls, and Rockcliff Falls are all accessible along Frank Coggins Trail #15 and Naturaland Trust Trail #14 at Caesars Head State Park.

Driving Directions:

1. From the Post Office in Cleveland follow US 276 West/SC 11 South for 5.1 miles to where US 276 turns right and SC 11 continues straight.

2. Turn right, staying on US 276, and continue 7.4 miles to Caesars Head State Park and the visitors center.

3. Park at the visitors center and cross US 276 to the trailhead.

Hiking Directions:

1. Hike 0.8 mile on Frank Coggins Trail #15 (purple blaze) to a footbridge at the top of Cliff Falls.

2. At this point, the Frank Coggins Trail connects with Rim of The Gap Trail #6 (yellow blaze) and Naturaland Trust Trail #14 (pink blaze).

3. Turn right onto Naturaland Trust Trail #14 and hike 0.3 mile to Firewater Falls.

4. Return on Naturaland Trust Trail #14 or continue 0.2 mile past the falls to US 276.

5. Turn right onto US 276 and walk 0.5 mile to the visitors center, completing a 2-mile loop.

Jones Gap Falls

Class:	Fan
Height:	50 feet
Rating:	Excellent
Stream:	Tributary of Middle Saluda River
Hike Length:	1.1 miles*
Hike Difficulty:	Moderate
Hiking Time:	1 hour*
USGS Quad:	Cleveland
Fee:	$2 per person

* one way

A pleasant hike on the well-maintained Jones Gap Trail #1 leads to Jones Gap Falls, which drops as a sheet of water over a rugged staircase of layered shelves and boulders, working its way downstream over many multi-colored ledges of granite.

The trail leading to Jones Gap Falls follows the boulder-strewn Middle Saluda River, a pleasant rushing stream that is in sight along most of the trail. A spur trail just past Campsite 11 leads directly to Jones Gap Falls. Several pools of water surrounded by large boulders in the Middle Saluda River provide refreshing wading areas.

Driving Directions:

1. From the Post Office in Cleveland, drive 1.1 miles on US 276 West/SC 11 South and turn right at the F-Mart convenience store onto River Falls Road.

2. Follow River Falls Road for 5.4 miles to the entrance of Jones Gap State Park and park in the lot on the right.

Hiking Directions:

1. Follow Jones Gap Trail #1 (blue blaze) for 0.9 mile upstream along the Middle Saluda River to the John Reid Clonts Memorial Bridge, a wooden footbridge.

2. Cross the Middle Saluda River on the footbridge and continue 0.1 mile to Campsite 11.

3. Follow a spur trail past Campsite 11 to the right (upstream) 150 feet to Jones Gap Falls.

HAIRY SPIDERWORT BUDS

Last Falls on Slickum Creek

Class:	Tiered
Height:	12 feet
Rating:	Nice
Stream:	Slickum Creek
Hike Length:	100 feet*
Hike Difficulty:	Easy
Hiking Time:	5 minutes*
USGS Quad:	Cleveland
Fee:	None

* one way

Located in upper Greenville County, 0.3 mile past Wildcat Falls, this waterfall is probably the last falls on Slickum Creek—thus the unofficial name. Slickum Creek crosses under US 276 through a metal culvert 100 feet downstream from this falls before emptying into the Saluda River.

This beautiful, 12-foot tiered falls begins with a twisting sluice at the upper level. The water rushes into a large pool suitable for wading and fishing.

My thanks to Bernie Boyer of Rosman, NC, for guiding me to this falls.

Driving Directions:

1. From the Post Office in Cleveland, drive 4.8 miles on US 276 West/SC 11 South (0.3 mile past the pulloff for Wildcat Falls.)

2. A metal culvert running under US 276 West/SC 11 South allows Slickum Creek to flow under the road and empty into the Saluda River. Pull off onto the right side of the road at this culvert.

Hiking Directions:

1. The unimproved trail begins at the left of the culvert.

2. Follow the trail paralleling the left side of Slickum Creek for 100 feet to the falls.

PINXTERFLOWER

Little Gilder Creek Falls

Class:	Tiered
Height:	10 feet
Rating:	Nice
Stream:	Little Gilder Creek
Hike Length:	Roadside
Hike Difficulty:	N/A
Hiking Time:	N/A
USGS Quad:	Cleveland
Fee:	None

Little Gilder Creek flows through the private River Walk Subdivision on Parkland Drive near Mauldin and Simpsonville, eventually flowing into Gilder Creek. Little Gilder Creek Falls is more like a shoals, with the water flowing over several layers of granite that form the bedrock of the creek. When the water is high and flowing fast, this falls resembles a rapid, with the water rushing over the different rock levels as the stream descends.

From the newly constructed stone bridge, the creek drops 10 feet over a distance of 200 feet before leveling off. This falls probably has no official name. For the purpose of listing it in this book, the name Little Gilder Creek Falls seems appropriate.

Driving Directions:

1. From Interstate 85 north of Greenville, take exit 51-A onto Woodruff Road, which is SC 146 East.

2. Follow Woodruff Road 3 miles to SC 14.

3. Turn right onto SC 14 and drive 1.6 miles to the intersection of Five Forks Road on the left.

4. Turn left onto Five Forks Road (SC 296) and go 500 feet to Parkland Drive on the right.

5. Turn right onto Parkland Drive and into River Walk Subdivision.

6. The falls are visible about 200 feet to the right, beginning under a bridge across Stonebridge Drive that marks the entrance into Avondale Heights Subdivision.

7. Note the signs indicating that parking is not permitted along Parkland Drive.

Hiking Directions:

There is no trail to the falls; they are visible from the roadside. The River Walk Subdivision contains 3 miles of paved trails for the exclusive use of the residents. If you know someone who lives in River Walk or Avondale Heights, they may invite you visit the falls and walk the trails.

RED MAPLE SEED

Mashbox Falls

Class:	Tiered
Height:	80 feet
Rating:	Good
Stream:	Tributary of Oil Camp Creek
Hike Length:	0.4 mile*
Hike Difficulty:	Strenuous
Hiking Time:	1 hour*
USGS Quad:	Cleveland
Fee:	None

* one way

Mashbox Falls has an interesting history. Located in upper Greenville County near Caesars Head State Park, this waterfall is situated in a steep hollow about 0.5 mile down the mountainside off SC 276, on a tributary of Oil Camp Creek. There is no access trail.

The falls is 80 feet high and flows over multiple tiers of large, flat boulders. The lower part is strewn with large boulders and trees that were washed downstream in the September 2004 hurricanes, Ivan and Frances.

Mashbox Falls is named for the metal box used to mix mash for moonshine. Measuring four feet by two feet by two feet, with handles on two sides so it can be moved, the box is sunk in the ground near the edge of the creek, about 300 feet from the base of the falls. Beside the mashbox are two 55-gallon water-filled drums, also sunk in the ground, that were probably used to cool the coils through which the liquid flowed and condensed in the moonshine-making process.

Mashbox Falls is separated by a ridge of about 0.2 mile from Misty Falls.

My thanks to Bob Julian of Easley, SC, for guiding me to this falls.

Driving Directions:

1. From the Post Office in Cleveland, follow US 276 West/SC 11 South 5.1 miles to the intersection where US 276 West turns right toward Caesars Head State Park.

2. Follow US 276 West for 5 miles to a narrow gravel road on the right. A man selling apples and honey is usually parked there in the summer.

3. Turn left onto the gravel road and park at a convenient place where the road is wide enough to turn around.

Hiking Directions:

1. Walk back up to US 276 and along the inside of the guardrail.

2. Near the end of the guardrail, begin a descent down the mountainside for about 0.2 mile toward the sound of the falls a little to the left.

3. There is no trail to the falls. Follow the sound of falling water, and if you come to Oil Camp Creek you will probably be downstream of the falls. Turn left and follow the creek upstream to the falls. There is no good way to give directions to this falls; the closer you get to Oil Camp Creek, the tributary, and the falls, the more difficult the bushwhacking because of downed trees.

VASSEY'S TRILLIUM

Misty Falls

Class:	Tiered
Height:	15 feet
Rating:	Good
Stream:	Tributary of Oil Camp Creek
Hike Length:	0.4 mile*
Hike Difficulty:	Strenuous
Hiking Time:	0.5 hour*
USGS Quad:	Cleveland
Fee:	None

* one way

Located near Caesars Head State Park in upper Greenville County, Misty Falls is a beautiful waterfall composed of multiple flat layers of rock outcrop in a deep ravine. The water drops several feet from one outcrop to the next, producing a misting effect around the falls.

The falls is situated on a tributary of Oil Camp Creek not far from Drip Rock Falls, on the side of SC 276 near Caesars Head State Park. There is no trail to this falls.

Misty Falls and Mashbox Falls are separated by only 0.2 mile over a ridge.

My thanks to Bob Julian of Easley, SC, for guiding me to this falls.

Driving Directions:

1. From the Post Office in Cleveland, follow US 276 West/SC 11 South 5.1 miles to the intersection where US 276 West turns right toward Caesars Head State Park.

2. Follow US 276 West for 5 miles to a narrow gravel road on the right. A man selling apples and honey is often parked there in the summer.

3. Turn left onto the gravel road and park at a convenient place where the road is wide enough to turn around.

Hiking Directions:

1. Walk back up to US 276 and along the inside of the guardrail for about half the length of the guardrail.

2. Descend the mountainside for about 0.2 mile toward the sound of the falls a little to the right.

3. There is no trail to the falls. Follow the sound of falling water, and if you come to Oil Camp Creek, you will probably be upstream of the falls. Turn right and follow the creek downstream. There is no good way to give directions to this falls; the closer you get to Oil Camp Creek, the tributary, and the falls, the more difficult the bushwhacking because of downed trees.

WHITE-TOPPED PITCHER PLANT

Misty Cavern Falls

Class:	Plunge
Height:	15 feet
Rating:	Good
Stream:	Unnamed
Hike Length:	1.7 miles*
Hike Difficulty:	Moderate
Hiking Time:	2.5 hours*
USGS Quad:	Cleveland
Fee:	$2 per person

* one way

Misty Cavern Falls is a low-volume plunge over a rock ledge located on Ishi Trail #8 in Jones Gap State Park. Behind the falls, which is situated in a massive cliff area alongside the trail, you can explore a large cavern littered with boulders.

The stream that feeds Misty Cavern Falls originates as springs and runoff from the upper part of the mountain above the cliffs. The amount of water flowing over the rock depends upon recent rainfall. An excellent time to view Misty Cavern Falls is in the winter when the water freezes into ten-foot-long icicles and sheets of ice that cover the boulders inside the cavern. Use extreme caution in the winter. In the spring of 2005 a hiker slipped and lost his life on the Ishi Trail. Always use caution on this difficult trail.

Driving Directions:

1. From the Post Office in Cleveland, drive 1.1 miles on US 276 West/SC 11 South and turn right at the F-Mart convenience store onto River Falls Road.

2. Follow River Falls Road for 5.4 miles to the entrance of Jones Gap State Park and park in the lot on the right.

Hiking Directions:

1. Follow Jones Gap Trail #1 (blue blaze) for 0.9 mile upstream along the Middle Saluda River to the John Reid Clonts Memorial Bridge, a wooden footbridge.

2. Ishi Trail #8 (white blaze) begins on the left before the footbridge and follows the Middle Saluda River upstream for a short distance.

3. Follow the Ishi Trail uphill away from the river for 0.8 mile to the caverns and cliffs on the right.

DOGWOOD

Moonshine Falls

Class:	Plunge
Height:	40 feet
Rating:	Excellent
Stream:	Tributary of Matthews Creek
Hike Length:	3 miles*
Hike Difficulty:	Moderate
Hiking Time:	3.5 hours*
USGS Quad:	Table Rock
Fee:	None

* one way

Moonshine Falls gets its name from the illegal activity carried on at the falls; remnants of old moonshining barrels remain in a cave behind its upper section. Because of a recent private land sale, the trail to Moonshine Falls has changed.

Located 1.5 miles downstream from Raven Cliff Falls, this waterfall plunges over a dark granite cliff as a narrow veil, then strikes a ledge, turns 90 degrees, and plunges into a deep pool. A spectacular view of the upper veil, the lower plunge, and the creek can be seen from behind the upper section of the falls.

The well-maintained trail originating at Asbury Hills Camp and Retreat Center, lined with mountain flora, makes this three-mile hike very enjoyable, and the beautiful waterfall destination makes the effort worthwhile.

The trails at Asbury Hills Camp and Retreat Center are open to the public. However, when the camp is in session from June 1 to the end of the first week in August, it is very crowded with young people and adults. During that time, please call the camp to find out if it is convenient to access the trails (see Appendix A for contact information).

Driving Directions:

1. From the Post Office in Cleveland, follow US 276 West/SC 11 South 5.1 miles to where US 276 West turns right toward Caesars Head State Park.

2. Follow US 276 West for 1.7 miles to Asbury Hills Camp and Retreat Center.

3. Turn left onto Lakemont Road at the entrance to Asbury Hills.

4. Immediately turn right and follow the road to a gate. Pass through the gate and continue 0.3 mile to the trailhead. This gate is locked at 5 pm.

5. Turn left just past the trailhead and park in the spaces on the left.

Hiking Directions:

1. Follow the Asbury Trail for 1.5 miles to a cable crossing over Matthews Creek. Continue on the Asbury Trail for 300 feet to where Naturaland Trust Trail #14 (pink blaze) connects.

2. Turn right onto Naturaland Trust Trail #14 and hike 0.5 mile to a right turn onto a trail that is partly blocked with a few tree limbs.

3. Continue 100 feet to an old kiosk, designated as a "Hot Spot," that indicates you are off Naturaland Trust Trail. Continue an easy hike from there.

4. Look for a small stack of rocks on the right with red paint marks indicating the spur trail to Moonshine Falls.

5. Turn right and continue 300 feet to a steep trail on the left that descends to the base of the falls.

New Millennium Falls—Lower

Class:	Waterslide
Height:	50 feet
Rating:	Good
Stream:	Slickum Creek
Hike Length:	0.5 mile*
Hike Difficulty:	Difficult
Hiking Time:	1 hour*
USGS Quad:	Cleveland
Fee:	None

* one way

The lower section of New Millennium Falls chain sits beside SC 276 near Wildcat Falls in upper Greenville County. This falls is 50 feet high and flows over a relatively flat section of a large rock outcrop.

The total hike distance to this falls is only 0.5 mile, but it is rated difficult because of the lack of an established trail; a large, bald, rocky outcrop that must be climbed over; and the bushwhacking required.

There are three separate sections in the New Millennium Falls chain, each separated by 0.1 mile on Slickum Creek. This falls probably has no official name but is called New Millennium because it was the first falls found by Norm Arnold and Phil Mayer after January 1, 2000, the beginning of the new millennium.

My thanks to Bernie Boyer of Rosman, NC, for guiding me to this falls.

Driving Directions:

1. From the Post Office in Cleveland, drive 4.5 miles on US 276 West/SC 11 South.

2. Park at Wildcat Falls, in the large roadside area on the right of US 276/SC 11, 0.6 mile before US 276 West turns right toward Caesars Head State Park.

Hiking Directions:

1. The trail to New Millennium Falls begins at the wooden stairs to the left of Lower Wildcat Falls.

2. Follow the well-maintained trail 0.1 mile to the intersection with a trail coming from the right.

3. Turn left at the intersection and follow the left side of a small stream upstream.

4. After 0.1 mile, the trail begins to climb and passes a large and long rock overhang. There is room for several campsites under the overhang and evidence of campfires.

5. Continue on the disappearing trail and enter a rocky area of small scrub pines, then veer slightly right to a large, bald, rock outcrop with patches of reindeer moss. You may see a few dark orange/red painted rectangles on the rock.

6. After crossing most of the bald rock area, you will hear the sound of a waterfall slightly to the left.

7. Bushwhack through some mountain laurel and you will emerge at the base of the two-tiered Upper New Millennium waterfall.

8. After working your way down to the Middle New Millennium waterfall, continue downstream on the left side of the stream.

9. You will emerge at the base of the large Lower New Millennium waterslide.

New Millennium Falls—Middle

Class:	Waterslide
Height:	18 feet
Rating:	Good
Stream:	Slickum Creek
Hike Length:	0.4 mile*
Hike Difficulty:	Strenuous
Hiking Time:	1 hour*
USGS Quad:	Cleveland
Fee:	None

* one way

The middle section of the New Millennium Falls chain is located in upper Greenville County beside SC 276 near Wildcat Falls. The falls is 18 feet high, and its thick sheet of water rushes over a large rounded and slick section of rock outcrop in a waterslide formation.

After bushwhacking to this section, you will arrive at the base of the waterslide. Due to large boulders and steep drop-offs in the creek, the only good place from which to get a photo is the side of the falls. Your first impression of this falls might remind you of heavy sweat streaming over the head of a bald man.

There are three separate sections in the New Millennium Falls chain, each separated by 0.1 mile on Slickum Creek. This falls probably has no official name but is called New Millennium because it was the first falls found by Norm Arnold and Phil Mayer after January 1, 2000, the beginning of the new millennium. The final section of the chain is just below this middle section.

My thanks to Bernie Boyer of Rosman, NC, for guiding me to this falls.

Driving Directions:

1. From the Post Office in Cleveland, drive 4.5 miles on US 276 West/SC 11 South.

2. Park at Wildcat Falls, in the large roadside area on the right of US 276/SC 11, 0.6 mile before US 276 West turns right toward Caesars Head State Park.

Hiking Directions:

1. The trail to New Millennium Falls begins at the wooden stairs to the left of Lower Wildcat Falls.

2. Follow the well-maintained trail 0.1 mile to the intersection with a trail coming from the right.

3. Turn left at the intersection and follow the left side of a small stream upstream.

4. After 0.1 mile, the trail begins to climb and passes a large and long rock overhang. There is room for several campsites under the overhang and evidence of campfires.

5. Continue on the disappearing trail and enter a rocky area of small scrub pines, then veer slightly right to a large, bald, rock outcrop with patches of reindeer moss. You may see a few dark orange/red painted rectangles on the rock.

6. After crossing most of the bald rock area, you will hear the sound of a waterfall slightly to the left.

7. Bushwhack through some mountain laurel and you will emerge at the base of the two-tiered Upper New Millennium waterfall.

8. Cross the creek at the base of the upper falls and go downstream to the top of the Middle New Millennium Falls.

9. Follow the side of the falls downstream on the left to the base of the falls.

New Millennium Falls—Upper

Class:	Tiered
Height:	25 feet
Rating:	Good
Stream:	Slickum Creek
Hike Length:	0.3 mile*
Hike Difficulty:	Strenuous
Hiking Time:	0.5 hour*
USGS Quad:	Cleveland
Fee:	None

* one way

The upper section of the New Millennium Falls chain is beside SC 276 near Wildcat Falls in upper Greenville County. This upper falls has two tiers, with a thick sheet of water rushing over large, slick bedrock in a small plunge to the lower section, which is more like a waterslide or shoal.

There are three separate sections in the New Millennium Falls chain, each separated by 0.1 mile on Slickum Creek. This falls probably has no official name but is called New Millennium because it was the first falls found by Norm Arnold and Phil Mayer after January 1, 2000, the beginning of the new millennium.

My thanks to Bernie Boyer of Rosman, NC, for guiding me to this falls.

Driving Directions:

1. From the Post Office in Cleveland, drive 4.5 miles on US 276 West/SC 11 South.

2. Park at Wildcat Falls in a large roadside area on the right of US 276/SC 11, 0.6 mile before US 276 West turns right toward Caesars Head State Park.

Hiking Directions:

1. The trail to all three levels of New Millennium Falls begins at the wooden stairs to the left of Lower Wildcat Falls.

2. Follow the well-maintained trail 0.1 mile to the intersection with a trail coming from the right.

3. Turn left at the intersection and follow the left side of a small stream upstream.

4. After 0.1 mile, the trail begins to climb and passes a large and long rock overhang. There is room for several campsites under the overhang and evidence of campfires.

5. Continue on the disappearing trail and enter a rocky area of small scrub pines, then veer slightly right to a large, bald, rock outcrop with patches of reindeer moss. You may see a few dark orange/red painted rectangles on the rock.

6. After crossing most of the bald rock area, you will hear the sound of a waterfall slightly to the left.

7. Bushwhack through some mountain laurel and you will emerge at the base of the two-tiered Upper New Millennium waterfall.

Oil Camp Falls

Class:	Tiered
Height:	70 feet
Rating:	Good
Stream:	Eastern Stream
Hike Length:	0.6 mile*
Hike Difficulty:	Moderate
Hiking Time:	1 hour*
USGS Quad:	Cleveland
Fee:	None

* one way

Oil Camp Falls is one of the cascades on Eastern Stream, which flows from the southern summit of Little Pinnacle Mountain in Jones Gap State Park. It drops over a 70-foot outcrop of rock to form a cataract bog before falling into Oil Camp Creek. The origin of Oil Camp Creek is Drip Rock Falls, located just south of Caesars Head State Park on US 276.

This short hike of 0.6 mile to Oil Camp Falls is worth the effort. After periods of heavy rain, especially in the spring, the flow of water can border on the spectacular.

Driving Directions:

1. From the Post Office in Cleveland, drive 1.1 miles on US 276 West/SC 11 South and turn right at the F-Mart convenience store onto River Falls Road.

2. Follow River Falls Road for 2.8 miles to Oil Camp Creek Road on the left.

3. Turn left onto Oil Camp Creek Road and drive 1.9 miles to where the pavement ends.

4. Follow the dirt road 0.1 mile to a small parking area.

Hiking Directions:

1. Walk around a green metal barricade and hike 0.5 mile to another metal barricade painted red.

2. Continue 0.1 mile to the bridge over Oil Camp Creek, passing Pinnacle Pass Trail #20 (orange blaze) on the right.

3. Cross the bridge and look for the falls on the right at 200 feet.

BEN GEER KEYS

WHITE OR LARGE-FLOWERED TRILLIUM

Pelham Falls

Class:	Tiered
Height:	15 feet
Rating:	Fair
Stream:	Rocky Creek
Hike Length:	Roadside
Hike Difficulty:	N/A
Hiking Time:	N/A
USGS Quad:	Pelham
Fee:	None

Although Pelham Falls has an established name as a waterfall, it is more a combination of rapids and shoals.

Located roadside and downstream from the bridge over SC 14, Pelham Falls drops 15 feet over a 200-foot stretch of multiple granite ledges in Rocky Creek near Pelham, SC. A pleasant pool with a sandy beach is at the base of the falls, and a calm creek flows through private property downstream.

Driving Directions:

1. From exit 56 on I-85 east of Greenville, SC, take SC 14 East, toward Pelham.

2. Follow SC 14 East for 1.7 miles to the bridge over Rocky Creek. The falls are downstream to the left of the bridge.

3. Turn left immediately past the bridge onto a private drive, then immediately left into a single-car parking space.

Hiking Directions:

There is no trail associated with this falls; it is visible from the bridge and from the parking space off the driveway. Fifty feet down the driveway on the left is a path to the shoreline. No Trespassing signs are posted on this private property.

ALUM ROOT

Pleasant Ridge Falls

Class:	Tiered
Height:	15 feet
Rating:	Fair
Stream:	Unnamed
Hike Length:	0.2 mile*
Hike Difficulty:	Easy
Hiking Time:	10 minutes*
USGS Quad:	Slater
Fee:	None

* one way

The double-tiered Pleasant Ridge Falls is located in Pleasant Ridge County Park on SC 11 in northern Greenville County, alongside the 0.7-mile Pleasant Ridge Nature Trail.

The upper tier drops 8 feet over a 25-foot stretch. The unnamed stream flows 20 feet from the first tier to begin the plunge over the 15-foot second tier, which is more picturesque.

A rustic bench made of a split tree trunk is conveniently placed at the upper level, affording a tranquil place to rest and observe the falls.

Driving Directions:

1. From Greenville, follow US 276 West to the intersection of SC 11.

2. Turn right onto SC 11 North and drive 2.5 miles to Pleasant Ridge State Park Road on the left.

3. Turn left onto Pleasant Ridge State Park Road.

4. Drive 0.7 mile to a parking area just before the office building at the swimming and boating lake.

Hiking Directions:

1. Walk from the parking lot along a short gravel road to the office building. A sign indicates the direction to the office and restrooms.

2. The trail begins behind the office building at a nature trail sign near a children's play area.

3. Follow the trail downhill over steps, rocks, and roots 100 feet to a T intersection.

4. Turn right at the intersection and hike 0.1 mile (crossing a wooden footbridge with handrails) to the falls on the left.

5. A left turn at the T intersection immediately takes you to a sign for an old moonshine still site.

Rainbow Falls

Class:	Plunge
Height:	140 feet
Rating:	Spectacular
Stream:	Cox Camp Creek
Hike Length:	0.5 mile*
Hike Difficulty:	Strenuous
Hiking Time:	1 hour*
USGS Quad:	Standingstone Mountain
Fee:	None

* one way

Plunging over a granite cliff surrounded by steep granite walls streaked with black and tan, Rainbow Falls is a richly rewarding sight for this strenuous hike. The 140-foot cascading thin ribbon of water sways in the wind as it plunges onto the granite boulders at its base.

This falls is secluded in a rugged gorge in northern Greenville County on Cox Camp Creek, on property owned by YMCA Camp Greenville. Upstream from Rainbow Falls on Cox Camp Creek is Shower Bath Falls.

Driving Directions:

1. From the Post Office in Cleveland, follow US 276 West/ SC 11 South for 5.1 miles to where US 276 turns right and SC 11 continues straight.

2. Turn right, staying on US 276, and continue 7.4 miles to Caesars Head State Park and the visitors center.

3. Follow US 276 West 2.6 miles past the park entrance and turn right onto Solomon Jones Road at the North Carolina state line. Watch for the Camp Greenville sign.

4. Follow Solomon Jones Road for 4.2 miles to a parking area at the YMCA Camp Greenville office.

5. Ask at the camp office for permission to walk to the falls.

Hiking Directions:

1. The trail begins on the right side of the road 0.2 mile from the camp office (ask for directions).

2. Follow the narrow, winding trail 0.5 mile to the base of the falls.

WILD GERANIUM

Raven Cliff Falls

Class:	Tiered
Height:	420 feet
Rating:	Spectacular
Stream:	Matthews Creek
Hike Length:	2.2 miles*
Hike Difficulty:	Moderate
Hiking Time:	2.5 hours*
USGS Quad:	Table Rock
Fee:	$2 per person

* one way

Raven Cliff Falls, on Matthews Creek in upper Greenville County, is one of the most scenic and photographed waterfalls in South Carolina. This falls was named for the ravens that breed in the high cliffs forming the falls. More than 150 species of ravens have been identified in this mountainous region. Views are available from three vantage points—two from the 2.2-mile Raven Cliff Trail #11, and the other from Dismal Trail #12, an additional distance of 0.1 mile.

Driving Directions:

1. From the Post Office in Cleveland follow US 276 West/SC 11 South for 5.1 miles to where US 276 turns right and SC 11 continues straight.

2. Turn right, staying on US 276, and continue 7.4 miles to Caesars Head State Park and the visitors center.

3. Follow US 276 West past Caesars Head State Park for 1.1 miles and turn right into the parking area designated for Raven Cliff Parking.

Hiking Directions:

1. Walk across US 276 to the trailhead and register at the kiosk.

2. Follow Raven Cliff Falls Trail #11 (red blaze) 1.4 miles to a T intersection at a kiosk.

3. At the T intersection turn left at the sign that indicates Raven Cliff Falls to the left and Foothills Trail to the right.

4. Continue 0.8 mile on Raven Cliff Falls Trail #11 (red blaze) to the observation platform across from the falls.

FALSE SOLOMON'S SEAL

Reedy River Falls

Class:	Block
Height:	28 feet
Rating:	Excellent
Stream:	Reedy River
Hike Length:	Roadside
Hike Difficulty:	N/A
Hiking Time:	N/A
USGS Quad:	Greenville
Fee:	None

Reedy River flows through Greenville, SC, making a spectacular 28-foot drop over the falls in the historic West End District of Greenville.

Greenville's unique Liberty Bridge (345 feet long and 12 feet wide) spans Reedy River above the Falls. This is the site where Greenville's first European settler, Richard Pearis, established his trading post in 1768. Later he built gristmills and sawmills at this location, which was the hub of industry in Greenville until the 1920s.

Driving Directions:

1. Located in the historic West End District of Greenville, SC, the roadside Reedy River Falls Historic Park is on South Main Street.
2. From I-85 (North or South), take I-385 to downtown Greenville.
3. Turn left onto Church Street.
4. Go right on East Camperdown Way.

Alternate Driving Directions:

1. From US 123 to Greenville, turn right onto South Main Street.
2. Go four blocks to Camperdown Way.

Hiking Directions:

1. Access to Reedy River Falls Historic Park is off the sidewalk on South Main Street.
2. An entranceway down rock steps leads to paved walkways throughout the park.

FAWN'S BREATH OR BOWMAN'S ROOT

Rock Quarry Falls

Class:	Tiered
Height:	10 feet
Rating:	Nice
Stream:	Rock Quarry Creek
Hike Length:	Roadside
Hike Difficulty:	Easy
Hiking Time:	N/A
USGS Quad:	Greenville
Fee:	None

Rock Quarry Falls, on the southwestern border of Cleveland Park in Greenville, SC, drops 10 feet over a sharp precipice into a small pool at the base. The sheer face of the rock over which the water cascades is the result of pre-Civil War quarry practices.

The Rock Quarry Garden near the waterfall has been developed and maintained through the cooperative efforts of the Greenville Garden Club and the City of Greenville's beautification staff. The area around the falls and the gardens is often reserved for weddings, photographs, and video advertising productions.

The stream running through the quarry flows from a spring on Spring Street that provided the water supply for many early Greenvillians.

Driving Directions:

1. Follow I-85 to exit 42. Turn onto I-385/US 29 North. US 29 soon becomes Mills Avenue.

2. Continue to the intersection with Augusta Street.

3. Turn right onto Augusta Street.

4. Follow Augusta Street for 0.6 mile to McDaniel Avenue at the traffic signal.

5. Turn left onto McDaniel Avenue.

6. Follow McDaniel Avenue for 1.1 miles to Ridgeland Drive.

7. Turn left onto Ridgeland Drive, then turn immediately right onto Sherwood Street.

8. Follow Sherwood Street for 100 feet to a small pulloff on the right at the stone steps leading into the quarry.

Hiking Directions:

There is no trail associated with this falls. As soon as you turn onto Sherwood Street, the falls is visible upstream to the right. A set of stone steps at the pulloff on Sherwood Street leads into the quarry and to the falls.

ORANGE DAISY

Rockcliff Falls

Class:	Sluice
Height:	40 feet
Rating:	Excellent
Stream:	Unnamed
Hike Length:	1.7 miles*
Hike Difficulty:	Moderate
Hiking Time:	1.5 hours*
USGS Quad:	Cleveland
Fee:	$2 per person

* one way

Rockcliff Falls is named for the massive rock outcrop over which it flows. The exposed cliff stretches 500 feet across the side of Caesars Head Mountain and is visible from US 276 before reaching Caesars Head State Park. The slant of the rock forms the narrow 40-foot sluice on the lower side of the outcrop.

Cliff Falls, Firewater Falls, and Rockcliff Falls are all accessible along Frank Coggins Trail #15 and Naturaland Trust Trail #14 at Caesars Head State Park.

Driving Directions:

1. From the Post Office in Cleveland, follow US 276 West/SC 11 South for 5.1 miles to where US 276 turns right and SC 11 continues straight.

2. Turn right, staying on US 276, and continue 7.4 miles to Caesars Head State Park and the visitors center.

3. Park at the visitors center and cross US 276 to the trailhead.

Hiking Directions:

1. Hike 0.8 mile on Frank Coggins Trail #15 (purple blaze) to a footbridge at the top of Cliff Falls.

2. At this point, Frank Coggins Trail connects with Rim of The Gap Trail #6 (yellow blaze) and Naturaland Trust Trail #14 (pink blaze).

3. Turn right onto Naturaland Trust Trail #14 and hike 0.3 mile to Firewater Falls on the right.

4. Continue 0.25 mile and cross US 276.

5. Continue on the trail parallel to the west side of US 276 for 0.2 mile to the Cliff Ridge Development.

6. Continue on the trail looking for pink blazes on rocks and trees and go through a boulder field.

7. The trail crosses a gravel driveway and descends 0.3 mile to the base of the falls.

8. Backtrack on the trail to US 276 and walk up the road 0.5 mile to the visitors center.

NOTE

The trail distance can be shortened by starting on the trail where it crosses US 276. Park at the visitors center and walk 0.5 mile down US 276 to the trail crossing.

Shower Bath Falls

Class:	Tiered
Height:	20 feet
Rating:	Good
Stream:	Cox Camp Creek
Hike Length:	0.2 mile*
Hike Difficulty:	Easy
Hiking Time:	20 minutes*
USGS Quad:	Eastatoe Gap
Fee:	None

* one way

Shower Bath Falls is one of the two waterfalls at YMCA Camp Greenville. It is a 20-foot plunge over two ledges on Cox Camp Creek, located 300 yards upstream from Rainbow Falls. Shower Bath Falls derives its name from the days before running water was available at Camp Greenville, and campers used these falls for their daily baths.

There is another trail leading down to the falls 50 feet farther along the road. This trail is the same length but much steeper. You can descend this trail to the falls and walk back up the easier trail.

Driving Directions:

1. From the Post Office in Cleveland follow US 276 West/ SC 11 South for 5.1 miles to where US 276 turns right and SC 11 continues straight.

2. Turn right, staying on US 276 and continue 7.4 miles to Caesars Head State Park and visitors center.

3. Follow US 276 West 2.6 miles past the park entrance and turn right onto Solomon Jones Road at the North Carolina state line. Watch for the Camp Greenville sign.

4. Follow Solomon Jones Road for 4.2 miles to a parking area at the Camp Greenville office.

5. Ask at the office for permission to walk to the falls.

Hiking Directions:

1. Take the road that curves to the right after passing the camp office.

2. Follow this road 200 feet from the camp office to the trailhead on the right.

3. Follow the narrow, winding trail 0.2 mile to the falls.

Slickum Falls

Class:	Waterslide
Height:	75 feet
Rating:	Good
Stream:	Slickum Creek
Hike Length:	0.25 mile*
Hike Difficulty:	Easy
Hiking Time:	15 minutes*
USGS Quad:	Cleveland
Fee:	None

* one way

Slickum Falls is a waterslide in the Eva Russell Chandler Heritage Trust Preserve in upper Greenville County. An easy 0.25-mile fern-lined trail leads past the remains of an old home site to an overlook where Slickum Falls cascades over a large rock outcrop, dropping 100 feet over a distance of 150 yards.

This falls is in an unusual ecological community known as a cataract bog. The moist soil in the bog supports many rare plants. The mountain sweet pitcher plant, a federally listed endangered species, is found in the Chandler Preserve and in only 39 other locations throughout the world. The massive exposed rock also has large areas of dense reindeer moss.

The complete trail is a half-mile loop leading from Persimmon Ridge Road past Slickum Falls and back to the road.

Driving Directions:

1. From the Post Office in Cleveland, follow US 276/SC 11 toward Caesars Head State Park for 3.2 miles to Persimmon Ridge Road on the right.

2. Follow Persimmon Ridge Road for 3 miles (paved for 0.3 mile, then gravel) to a parking area and trailhead on the left. A large sign identifies this as the Eva Russell Chandler Heritage Trust Preserve.

Hiking Directions:

1. The trail begins at the parking area behind a metal gate at the sign for the Eva Russell Chandler Heritage Trust Preserve.

2. Follow the roadbed 200 feet to a left turn.

3. Turn left onto the narrow trail and ascend a small set of steps.

4. Pass an old chimney on the right and proceed to the overlook on the right at the top of the falls.

5. The trail continues another 0.2 mile to Persimmon Ridge Road.

6. Turn left on the road and continue 300 feet to the parking area.

INDIAN PIPE

Sweet Thing on Slickum

Class:	Plunge
Height:	18 feet
Rating:	Excellent
Stream:	Slickum Creek
Hike Length:	0.2 mile*
Hike Difficulty:	Easy
Hiking Time:	15 minutes*
USGS Quad:	Cleveland
Fee:	None

* one way

Sweet Thing On Slickum Creek is hidden in a Slickum Creek grotto in upper Greenville County, 0.3 mile past Wildcat Falls.

This waterfall is a beautiful 18-foot plunge over a hollowed-out rock ledge into a large, deep pool. The semi-circular cave behind the falls is large enough to walk through. The ensuing stream levels out below into several small pools for wading or fishing.

My thanks to Bernie Boyer of Rosman, NC, for guiding me to this falls.

Driving Directions:

1. From the Post Office in Cleveland, drive 4.8 miles on US 276 West/SC 11 South (0.3 mile past the pulloff for Wildcat Falls.)

2. Pull off onto the right side of the road at the metal culvert that runs under US 276 West/SC 11 South.

Hiking Directions:

1. The trail to Sweet Thing on Slickum Creek begins at the left of the culvert.

2. Follow the unimproved trail paralleling the left side of Slickum Creek for 0.2 mile, passing Last Falls on Slickum Creek on the way to Sweet Thing.

YELLOW ASTOR

Walking Fern Falls

Class:	Waterslide
Height:	80 feet
Rating:	Good
Stream:	Walking Fern Creek
Hike Length:	1.1 miles*
Hike Difficulty:	Moderate
Hiking Time:	1.5 hours*
USGS Quad:	Cleveland
Fee:	$2 per person

* one way

Walking Fern Falls is not a major waterfall, but it is an interesting place to relax while hiking Pinnacle Pass Trail #20. The falls is a low-volume waterslide at least 80 feet high which is visible from the trail. It is named for the rare Walking Fern found in the area. Wherever a frond of the Walking Fern touches the ground, a new fern begins to grow. Thus the fern "walks" across the ground and propagates itself.

The remains of an old moonshine still, including two rusted drums and heavy pipes, are scattered around the area, as shown in the foreground of the photo.

One mile beyond Walking Fern Falls, the trail drops down onto a rock abutment for an incredible view of Jones Gap.

Driving Directions:

1. From the Post Office in Cleveland, drive 1.1 miles on US 276 West/SC 11 South and turn right at the F-Mart convenience store onto River Falls Road.

2. Follow River Falls Road 5.4 miles to the entrance of Jones Gap State Park and park in the lot on the right.

Hiking Directions:

1. Follow Jones Gap Trail #1 (blue blaze) upstream for 300 feet to where it intersects Rim of The Gap Trail #6 (yellow blaze).

2. Turn left onto Rim of The Gap Trail and continue for 0.4 mile to Pinnacle Pass Trail #20 (orange blaze), which begins at a small creek.

3. Follow Pinnacle Pass Trail 0.6 mile to Walking Fern Falls.

WALKING FERN

Wildcat Falls—Lower

Class:	Tiered
Height:	30 feet
Rating:	Good
Stream:	Wildcat Branch
Hike Length:	Roadside
Hike Difficulty:	N/A
Hiking Time:	N/A
USGS Quad:	Cleveland
Fee:	None

Wildcat Falls often goes unnoticed by the casual tourist hurrying by on US 276/SC 11. This waterfall has three levels, with heights as follows: the lower level–30 feet; the middle level–10 feet; and the upper level–100 feet.

The lower falls, also know as Wildcat Wayside Falls, is visited by children and adults who wade and play in the calm pool at the base. A cross has been placed beside the lower pool in memory of a life lost on this falls.

Driving Directions:

1. From the Post Office in Cleveland, drive 4.5 miles on US 276 West/SC 11 South.

2. Park in the large paved area on the right side of US 276/SC 11, 0.6 mile before the US 276 West turns right toward Caesars Head State Park.

Hiking Directions:

There is no trail associated with the lower falls. It is roadside and can be observed from the pulloff.

BIRDFOOT VIOLET

Wildcat Falls—Middle

Class:	Plunge
Height:	10 feet
Rating:	Good
Stream:	Wildcat Branch
Hike Length:	0.1 mile*
Hike Difficulty:	Easy
Hiking Time:	5 minutes*
USGS Quad:	Cleveland
Fee:	None

* one way

Wildcat Falls has three levels: the lower level–30 feet in height; the middle level–10 feet; and the upper level–100 feet. The middle level of Wildcat Falls is 0.1 mile upstream from the lower section, which is located on US 276/SC 11. The two sections are linked by a pleasant rippling stream.

Some consider this section the top of Lower Wildcat Falls, but there is enough distance between it and the lower section for it to stand on its own as a waterfall.

Driving Directions:

1. From the Post Office in Cleveland, drive 4.5 miles on US 276 West/SC 11 South.

2. Park in the large paved area on the right, 0.6 mile before US 276 West makes a right toward Caesars Head State Park.

Hiking Directions:

1. The trail to the middle falls begins at the wooden stairs to the left of the lower falls.

2. Follow the well-maintained trail 0.1 mile to the middle falls.

Yellow Trumpet

Wildcat Falls—Upper

Class:	Tiered
Height:	100 feet
Rating:	Excellent
Stream:	Wildcat Branch
Hike Length:	0.4 mile*
Hike Difficulty:	Moderate
Hiking Time:	0.5 hour*
USGS Quad:	Cleveland
Fee:	None

* one way

Wildcat Falls has three levels: the lower level–30 feet in height; the middle level–10 feet; and the upper level–100 feet. The most spectacular of the three sections, the upper level flows over a 100-foot rock ledge with massive boulders at its base. It is located 0.3 mile upstream from the middle section.

The trail to the upper falls is easy until it reaches the boulders, but climbing over them is quite difficult—and is illegal since many accidents, deaths, and difficult rescues forced the South Carolina State Park Service to make the upper falls off limits. (Signs prohibiting hiking to the upper falls have been vandalized.) Fortunately, an excellent view of the upper falls is possible without crossing the boulders.

Driving Directions:

1. From the Post Office in Cleveland, drive 4.5 miles on US 276 West/SC 11 South.

2. Park in the large paved roadside area on the right, 0.6 mile before US 276 makes a right turn toward Caesars Head State Park.

Hiking Directions:

1. The trail to the upper falls begins at the wooden stairs to the left of the lower falls.

2. Follow the well-maintained trail 0.4 mile to the base of the upper falls.

3. Be aware that the trail to Upper Wildcat Falls is closed to the public.

HEPATICA

Waterfalls
of
North Carolina & Georgia

WHITEWATER FALLS—UPPER

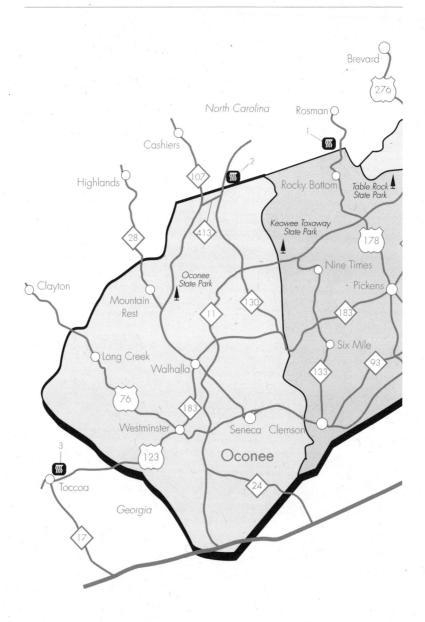

Three waterfalls in North Carolina and Georgia are so close and so beautiful that they must be included with the Upstate South Carolina waterfalls. Eastatoe Falls is only a few miles across the North Carolina state line, and Toccoa Falls, a major attraction in northern Georgia, is only a few miles across the Georgia state line. Upper Whitewater Falls in North Carolina is so close to the state line that many people believe it is in South Carolina.

BEN GEER KEYS

TURK'S CAP LILY

Eastatoe Falls

Class:	Tiered
Height:	70 feet
Rating:	Excellent
Stream:	Shoal Creek
Hike Length:	0.1 mile*
Hike Difficulty:	Easy
Hiking Time:	10 minutes*
USGS Quad:	Eastatoe Gap
Fee:	None

* one way

Eastatoe Falls is on private land in the Eastatoe Community in North Carolina, a short distance from the Upstate area north of SC 11. Please respect this private residential property.

The falls flows 70 feet over multiple granite ledges onto large boulders and huge blown-down trees. A pleasant, calm stream continues from the base of the falls.

Eastatoe was the Cherokee name for the Carolina Parakeet. The Eastatoe tribe of the Cherokees, known as the "Green Bird People," used the colorful green and yellow feathers to adorn ceremonial robes. The Carolina Parakeet, once abundant in the Carolinas, has been extinct since the mid-1900s.

Driving Directions:

1. From Pickens, follow US 178 West for 8.6 miles to SC 11.

2. Cross SC 11 and follow US 178 West another 13.1 miles and look for a small sign on the left for the Mountain Meadow Craft Shop.

3. Turn left at the sign between two ponds and park between the craft shop and the private residence. The craft shop is no longer in operation, and the parking area is actually part of the circular drive around the residence.

Hiking Directions:

The trail begins at the craft shop and is a slight uphill walk of 0.1 mile. The falls is on private residential property. Get permission from the property owner to park in the driveway and visit the falls.

YELLOW PITCHER PLANT

Toccoa Falls

Class:	Plunge
Height:	186 feet
Rating:	Spectacular
Stream:	Toccoa Creek
Hike Length:	100 yards*
Hike Difficulty:	Easy
Hiking Time:	2 minutes*
USGS Quad:	Toccoa
Fee:	$1 per person

* one way

Toccoa Falls is located in Toccoa, GA, on the campus of Toccoa Falls College. This falls is 10 feet higher than Niagara Falls and the highest free-falling waterfall east of the Mississippi River. The Cherokee Indian word, "Toccoah," means "beautiful," and Toccoa Falls is well named.

Early on the Sunday morning of November 6, 1977, a severe rainstorm dropped nine inches of water, causing an earthen dam above the falls to collapse. A violent torrent poured over the falls, taking with it large boulders from the top. Thirty-nine people were killed and hundreds more on the campus were injured. A granite memorial marker engraved with the names of the deceased stands at the base of the falls. The physical structure of the falls was changed forever on that fateful day, not to mention the destiny of many people.

Driving Directions:

1. From the SC/GA line, take I-85 South to the Lavonia/Toccoa exit.

2. Keep left at the fork in the ramp.

3. Turn left onto GA 17. Continue straight on this road as it becomes Big-A Road, which curves to the left and becomes Tugalo Street.

4. Go straight through 3 traffic lights.

5. At the next intersection turn right onto Alexander Street.

6. After 1 mile turn left onto the Toccoa Falls College campus, marked by a large gray brick sign on the left.

7. Follow the signs on campus to the Gate Cottage Gift Shop.

Hiking Directions:

1. Access to the trail is through the Gate Cottage Gift Shop.

2. Exit a rear door of the gift shop onto the 100-yard trail to the base of the falls.

Whitewater Falls—Upper

Class:	Tiered
Height:	411 feet
Rating:	Spectacular
Stream:	Whitewater River
Hike Length:	600 feet*
Hike Difficulty:	Easy
Hiking Time:	10 minutes*
USGS Quad:	Reid
Fee:	$2 per vehicle

* one way

Whitewater Falls, located north of Salem, SC, just across the North Carolina border on the Whitewater River, is a set of two major falls. The spectacular plunge of 411 feet makes Upper Whitewater Falls the tallest waterfall east of the Mississippi River. South Carolina's Lower Whitewater Falls drops another 200 feet. The entire Whitewater Falls chain consists of six different waterfalls along the North and South Carolina line, plunging nearly 700 feet for more than half a mile before emptying into Lake Jocassee.

A sign at the viewing area lists 26 hikers who lost their lives in accidents at Upper Whitewater Falls.

Driving Directions:

1. From Walhalla, follow SC 28 West for 8.1 miles and bear right onto SC 107 North.
2. Follow SC 107 North 13.9 miles to Wigington Road (SC 413) on the right.
3. Turn right onto Wigington Road and proceed 2.2 miles to the intersection of SC 130.
4. Turn left onto SC 130 and proceed 1.1 miles to the entrance to Whitewater Falls on the right.

Hiking Directions:

1. An asphalt trail ascends 600 feet from the parking lot past picnic shelters to the first viewing area of the falls at the end of the asphalt trail.
2. At a wooden split-rail fence at the top of the asphalt trail, a series of steps—12 sections, with a total of approximately 150 steps—descends at the right to a viewing platform.

Alternate Driving Directions:

1. From the junction of US 76/ SC 28 at Seneca, turn onto SC 130.
2. Stay on SC 130 for 8.7 miles to the intersection of SC 183.
3. Stay on SC 130 for another 9.3 miles (passing through Salem) to the intersection with SC 11.
4. Cross SC 11 and proceed 10.5 miles to the entrance of Whitewater Falls on the right.

Appendices

Brasstown falls veil

Waterfalls, Ions, and Prozac

Backpackers understand the fascination [of waterfalls]. When a bend in the trail reveals a torrent in freefall, we're struck dumb by wonder. Even the quiet burbling of a small stream exerts a seductive, hypnotic attraction.

"I have an obsession going with waterfalls," admits Bryan Swan, 20, of Bellevue, WA. As a hiker and web master for the Pacific Northwest Waterfall Database (www.wpnw.addr.com/pnwd/index.html), Swan estimates he's visited 425 falls in the Northwest alone, and suspects his overall tally might be 700.

"Waterfalls are like snowflakes—no two are alike," Swan contends. "And you get that charge when you go in there. I can't put a finger on the exact attraction, but there's a primal force you can't get anywhere else."

Turns out there's some weird science to explain the attraction. Sun, lightning, seashore waves, and waterfalls all create electrically charged particles called ions. Scientists credit negatively charged atmospheric ions, a by-product of misting water, with the fresh feel of clean air. They've also been found to calm moods by altering the brain's serotonin levels in much the same way that Prozac does. Waterfalls produce negative ions in abundance; the concentration near a pounding cascade is 5,000 times that of an office or on a city street, and hundreds of times higher than sea or lakeshores.

The bottom line to all this biochemistry is that there are few things so uplifting as a wild waterfall.

—backpacker.com

Appendix A:

Important Addresses and Telephone Numbers

- Asbury Hills Camp
  150 Asbury Drive
  Cleveland, SC 29635
  864-836-3711

- Caesars Head State Park
  8155 Geer Highway
  Cleveland, SC 29635
  864-836-6115

- Chau Ram County Park
  1220 Chau Ram Park Road
  Westminster, SC 29693
  864-647-9286

- Falls Park
  601 South Main Street
  Greenville, SC 29601
  864-467-4355

- Jones Gap State Park
  303 Jones Gap Road
  Marietta, SC 29661
  864-836-3647

- Keowee-Toxaway State Natural Area
  108 Residence Drive
  Sunset, SC 29685
  864-868-2605

- Oconee Station State Historic Site
  500 Oconee Station Road
  Walhalla, SC 29691
  864-638-0079

- Oconee State Park
  624 State Park Road
  Mountain Rest, SC 29664
  864-638-5353

- Sumter National Forest
  Andrew Pickens Ranger District
  112 Andrew Pickens Circle
  Mountain Rest, SC 29664
  864-638-9568

- Toccoa Falls College
  Toccoa Falls, GA 30598
  706-886-6831

- YMCA Camp Greenville
  PO Box 390
  Cedar Mountain, NC 28718
  864-836-3291

Appendix B:

Waterfall Hubs

A hub is a grouping of waterfalls located within a defined geographical area. Knowing that several waterfalls are near each other aids in planning trips to groups of falls. The hubs listed in this book are central points such as a city or along a major highway or near a state park.

• Oconee County Hubs

Highway 107 Hub: 17 Waterfalls

Oconee State Park Hub: 3 Waterfalls

▪ Pickens County Hubs

▪ Greenville County Hubs

Bibliography

- Adams, Kevin. *North Carolina Waterfalls: A Hiking and Photography Guide.* John F. Blair, Winston-Salem, NC: 2005. 590 pages.

- Adams, Kevin. *North Carolina Waterfalls: Where to Find Them, How to Photograph Them.* John F. Blair, Winston-Salem, NC: 2003. 208 pages.

- Arnold, Norm. *Waterfalls Near Our Home in Keowee Key, SC.* 1995. 39 pages.

- Arnold, Norm. *Waterfalls Near Our Home in Keowee Key, SC, Book II.* 1997. 21 pages.

- Blagden, Tom, Jr., and Thomas Wyche. *South Carolina's Mountain Wilderness, The Blue Ridge Escarpment.* Westcliffe Publishers, Englewood, CO: 1994. 128 pages.

- Ballenger, Sidney Holmes, Jr., John E. Danner, and Maxie W. Duke. *Some Waterfalls, Cascades, and Shoals in Oconee County, South Carolina.* Walhalla, SC, 1983. Unpublished notebook at Stumphouse Ranger Station and Walhalla Public Library, giving height, creek, USGS quadrangle map, and photo for 65 falls.

- Boyd, Brian. *Waterfalls of the Southern Appalachians and Great Smoky Mountains,* 4th ed. Fern Creek Press, Clayton, GA: 2001. 160 pages.

- Brooks, Benjamin, and Tim Cook. *The Waterfalls of South Carolina,* 2nd ed. Palmetto Conservation Foundation, Spartanburg, SC: 2001. 78 pages.

- *Camper's Guide to YMCA Camp Greenville.* Brochure.

- de Hart, Allen. *Hiking South Carolina Trails,* 5th ed. Globe Pequot Press, Chester, CT: 2001. 341 pages.

- *Favorite Family Hikes.* Palmetto Conservation Foundation Press, Spartanburg, SC. 2004. 86 pages.

- *Finding the Falls: A Guide to Twenty-Five of the Upstate's Outstanding Waterfalls.* South Carolina Wildlife and Marine Resources Department and South Carolina Department of Parks, Recreation, and Tourism. Color brochure: 25 falls with descriptions and directions. 1992, revised 1994.

- *The Foothills Trail: A Comprehensive Guide.* Foothills Trail Conference. 1998. 110 pages.

- *History of Meece Mill.* Booklet available at Meece Mill. Pickens, SC. 2003.

- *Jocassee Journal.* South Carolina Department of Natural Resources, Pendleton, SC. Fall/Winter 2005, 16 pages; Fall/Winter 2006, 12 pages.

- *Keowee-Toxaway State Natural Area.* Brochure available at Keowee-Toxaway State Park.

- Keys, Ben Geer. *Natural Images of the Southern Appalachians.* Keys Printing, Greenville, SC: 1999. 128 pages.

- *Liberty Bridge.* Brochure from Falls Park, Greenville, SC.

- Morrison, Mark. *Waterfall Walks and Drives in the Great Smoky Mountains and the Western Carolinas.* H. F. Publishing, Douglasville, GA: 1999. 158 pages.

- *Mountain Bridge Trails,* 3rd ed. Naturaland Trust, Greenville, SC: 1998. 254 pages.

- *Oconee Connector of the Palmetto Trail.* Palmetto Conservation Foundation. Brochure.

- Oeland, Glenn. "Falling Waters." *South Carolina Wildlife.* July-August 1990, pp. 28-41. (Available from *South Carolina Wildlife* Magazine, PO Box 167, Columbia, SC 29202.)

- Tagliapietra, Ron. *150 South Carolina Waterfalls.* Fern Creek Press, Clayton, GA: 2000. 80 pages.

- Tagliapietra, Ron. *Waterfalls of the States.* Fern Creek Press, Clayton, GA: 2002. 234 pages.

- *Toccoa Falls.* Toccoa Falls College. Brochure.

- *Tour Pickens County South Carolina.* Pickens County Council and the Chambers of Commerce of Clemson, Easley, Liberty, and Pickens County. Pickens, SC. 2005. 31 pages.

- U.S. Department of Agriculture, Forest Service. *Trail Construction and Maintenance Notebook.* 9623-2833-MTDC. Washington, DC: U.S. Department of Agriculture, Forest Service, 1997. 139 pages.

- *Waterfalls of the South Carolina Upcountry.* South Carolina Department of Natural Resources. Brochure.

- *Waterfalls of the Sumter National Forest.* Unpublished notebook at Stumphouse Ranger Station, Oconee County, SC.

- Wyche, Thomas. *Mosaic: 21 Special Places in the Carolinas.* Westcliffe Publishers, Englewood, CO: 2002. 94 pages.

- Wyche, Thomas, and James Kilgo. *The Blue Wall: Wilderness of the Carolinas and Georgia,* Westcliffe Publishers, Englewood, CO: 1996. 112 pages.

Web sites

- Carolina Mountain Club. www.carolinamtnclub.com

- Francis Marion and Sumter National Forests. USDA Forest Service. www.fs.fed.us/r8/fms/forest/recreation/waterfalls.shtml

- Local Hikes. www.localhikes.com/MSA/MSA_3160.asp

- SCwaterfalls.com. www.alleneasler.com/waterfalls.html

- USDA, NRCS. 2005. *PLANTS Database*, Version 3.5. www.plants.usda.gov. Data compiled from various sources by Mark W. Skinner. National Plant Data Center, Baton Rouge, LA 70874-4490 USA.

- Wildflowers of the Southern Appalachian Mountains. Darryl Goodman. www.wncwildflowers.com

- Wildflowers of the Southern Appalachian Mountains, Trees and Shrubs. Darryl Goodman. www.geocities.com/deekaygoodman/treesandshrubs.html

Acknowledgments

I must first acknowledge the Creator of the Earth and all that is in it. Beautiful waterfalls show us God's power and glory.

In the beginning God created the heaven and the earth... and God saw that it was good. Genesis 1:1, 10

The heavens declare the glory of God; and the firmament sheweth his handywork. Psalm 19:1

Deep calleth unto deep at the noise of thy waterspouts: all thy waves and thy billows are gone over me. Psalm 42:7

I also wish to thank the dedicated authors, hikers, and photographers who have published many excellent trail and waterfall guides. Many of these publications were used as sources for data in this work. Every attempt has been made to give credit to these sources in the bibliography. Several Internet sites containing trail and waterfall information were also used.

About the Author

Tom King was born in Anderson, South Carolina and has been an avid hiker and backpacker all his life. Long before established trails were commonplace, he was hiking along the Chattooga River in northwestern South Carolina, throughout the Sumter National Forest, and in Table Rock State Park. He followed trail markings on topographical maps and practiced the "leave no trace" ethic before it became widely known. His love of photography, especially nature photography, has won him prizes in several local contests and a state-sponsored contest by the South Carolina Department of Parks, Recreation, and Tourism.

Tom conducts guided hikes along trails and to waterfalls for individuals and groups. Using his background in accounting and real estate appraisal, he teaches the wise use and development of our land as a commodity, recognizing the great importance of preserving it as a resource for future generations.

Tom lives in Anderson County, South Carolina, with his wife Fay. He has introduced his two granddaughters, Kaitlin and Ashley, to the thrill of the trail, the splendor of Upstate waterfalls, and the pleasure of wading and splashing in cold, calm mountain pools. Through his photography and descriptions of waterfall hikes he encourages everyone to journey into the pristine wilderness of Upstate South Carolina and experience its splendid waterfalls.

Milestone Press

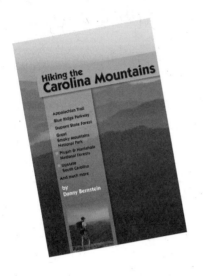

Hiking

- *Hiking the Carolina Mountains* by Danny Bernstein

- *Hiking North Carolina's Blue Ridge Heritage* by Danny Bernstein

- *Waterfalls Hikes of Upstate South Carolina* by Thomas E. King

Rockhounding
by Michael Streeter

- *A Rockhounding Guide to North Carolina's Blue Ridge Mountains*

Can't find the Milestone Press book you want at a bookseller near you? Don't despair—you can order it directly from us. Call us at 828-488-6601 or shop online at www.milestonepress.com.

Motorcycle Adventure Series
by Hawk Hagebak

- *1–Southern Appalachians North GA, East TN, Western NC*

- *2–Southern Appalachians Asheville, NC, Blue Ridge Parkway, NC Highcountry*

- *3–Central Appalachians Virginia's Blue Ridge, Shenandoah Valley, West Virginia Highlands*

Off the Beaten Track Mountain Bike Series
by Jim Parham

- *Vol. 1: WNC–Smokies*
- *Vol. 2: WNC–Pisgah*
- *Vol. 3: N. Georgia*
- *Vol. 4: E. Tennessee*
- *Vol. 5: N. Virginia*

Milestone Press

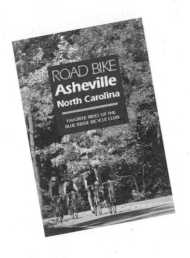

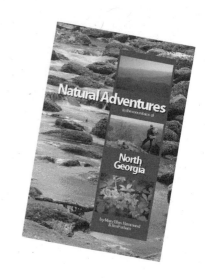

Road Bike Series

- *Road Bike Asheville, NC: Favorite Rides of the Blue Ridge Bicycle Club* by The Blue Ridge Bicycle Club

- *Road Bike the Smokies: 16 Great Rides in NC's Great Smoky Mountains* by Jim Parham

- *Road Bike North Georgia: 25 Great Rides in the Mountains and Valleys of North Georgia* by Jim Parham

Family Adventure
by Mary Ellen Hammond & Jim Parham

- *Natural Adventures in the Mountains of North Georgia*

Playboating
by Kelly Fischer

- *Playboating the
  Nantahala River—
  An Entry Level Guide*

Can't find the Milestone Press book you want at a bookseller near you?
Don't despair—you can order it directly from us. Call us at
828-488-6601 or shop online at www.milestonepress.com.